All Things in Common

All Things in Common

The Economic Practices of the Early Christians

ROMAN A. MONTERO

Foreword by Edgar G. Foster

RESOURCE *Publications* · Eugene, Oregon

ALL THINGS IN COMMON
The Economic Practices of the Early Christians

Resource Publications
An Imprint of Wipf and Stock Publishers
199 W. 8th Ave., Suite 3
Eugene, OR 97401

www.wipfandstock.com

PAPERBACK ISBN: 978-1-5326-0791-2
HARDCOVER ISBN: 978-1-5326-0793-6
EBOOK ISBN: 978-1-5326-0792-9

Manufactured in the U.S.A.   MARCH 6, 2019

Contents

Foreword

ACADEMICS CLASSIFY ECONOMICS AS a social science along with psychology, anthropology, sociology, and history; the social sciences usually are distinguished from the so-called hard sciences like physics, chemistry, biology or astronomy. Nevertheless, Biblical scholars (among others) have found value in using the social sciences with the aim of illuminating scriptural texts and their respective sociocultural contexts. One can point to studies written by Malina, Pilch,[1] and Osiek.[2] The last-mentioned study offers some cautionary advice for scholars who choose to use social-scientific approaches in their work, and Osiek issues the reminder that the social sciences have their individual strengths and concomitant weaknesses. For example, economics like any other discipline, only models what transpires in the actual world: scientific models do not wholly correspond to things and events in the world. Einstein writes: "As far as the laws of *mathematics* refer to reality, they are not *certain*, and as far as they are *certain*, they do not refer to reality." Modeling only approximates reality as opposed to identically mirroring the external world.

The tentative or provisional nature of economic models is not the only thing that Osiek discusses; yet another concern for some is the Marxist foundation of social sciences. The "father of sociology" is Auguste Comte. He originated the term "sociology" and proffered the view that society unfolded in three stages—religious, metaphysical, and scientific. Comte

---

1. Malina and Pilch, *Social Science Commentary on the Book of Revelation*; Malina, *The New Jerusalem in the Revelation of John.*

2. Osiek, "The Social Sciences and the Second Testament," 88–95.

insisted that the religious and metaphysical stages depended on non-rigorous and unsatisfactory methods to account for social phenomena, so they lacked genuine explanatory power. He advanced the suggestion that neither religion nor metaphysics have the efficacious potency to account for social phenomena. Hence, Comte proposed that sociologists would eventually develop a scientific approach that would surpass the other two stages with respect to explanatory potency. It is easy to ascertain the elements of positivism at play with Comte's approach since he privileged empiricism, statistics and evolutionary thought. Positivism elevates the quantifiable or focuses on what is measurable, and it supposedly operates without the usual biases of other methods. Nevertheless, opponents of positivism say that no facts are unfiltered: we all start with specific preapprehensions.

The founder of sociology pioneered the way for Marxist conflict theory; Karl Marx consequently shaped his own thought to revolve around class conflict, economic stages, and revolution.[3] G.W.F. Hegel, a German idealist, who enjoyed iconic status at the University of Berlin, provided the elements that Marx apparently needed to develop a comprehensive theory of history and class conflict.[4] But while Hegel portrayed the Weltgeist abstractly or ideally unfolding throughout history by means of a triadic dialectical movement (thesis, antithesis, and synthesis, as it were), Marx understood history's dialectical progression to occur by dint of economic changes, that is, via alterations whereby one type of economic system leads to another opposing system, which ultimately culminates in a classless society wherein *"From each according to his ability*, to *each according to his needs"* becomes the applicable and governing slogan. Marx asserted: "In a higher phase of communist society, after the enslaving subordination of the individual to the division of labor, and therewith also the antithesis between mental and physical labor, has vanished; after labor has become not only a means of life but life's prime want; after the productive forces have also increased with the all-around development of the individual, and all the springs of co-operative wealth flow more abundantly," then each would give from his ability "to each according to his needs."

Marxian thought has exercised great influence in China, North Korea, Cuba, and the former Soviet Union. Keith Ward considers elements of this

---

3. Marx has been described as "the greatest critical theorist of the Industrial Revolution and nineteenth-century capitalism." Stevenson, Haberman, and Wright, *Twelve Theories of Human Nature*, 187.

4. Ward, *The Case for Religion*, 64.

philosophy to be "both theoretically dubious and highly value-laden" and possibly "wish-fulfilling."[5] Contra the teachings of Jesus, Marx appeared to emphasize humanity's limitless ability to produce ideal circumstances (rather than looking to God's sovereign rule); all we need are the right conditions to make social environments flourish. Nonetheless, a theory like Marxism that stresses human potency and creaturely governance clashes head-on with the Christian doctrine of sin, on one hand, and divine omnipotence from another perspective. Only God is able to bring about liberation, not the creature. Ward also contends that Marxian theory potentially fails on two other fronts: 1) Human life is characterized by aggression and avid desire; 2) Marxist governments have been tried and found wanting. Of course, there are possible responses to these criticisms, but the important question is whether "communitarianism" in the relevant sense is feasible within a Christian setting.

Marxism and Christianity seem to be diametrical opposites: hardly anyone disputes that point. So is it possible to redeem elements of this philosophy so that it becomes applicable for communities like the ancient Christian ecclesia? Roman A. Montero's work *All Things in Common* makes an interesting proposal by employing the famous Marxist slogan as a springboard for discussing practices of the early Christian congregation, concerning which Luke narrates in Acts of the Apostles; however, Montero argues that while Marx might have articulated the slogan, "*From each according to his ability,* to *each according to his needs,*" there is evidence that early Christians somehow lived by the slogan since Luke reports that certain followers of Jesus held all things in common with one another following Pentecost (Acts 2:44; 4:32). Montero invokes history and economics in the process of setting forth an arresting narrative. Yet how does he contribute to the growing use of social-scientific approaches in Biblical studies?

The aforementioned proposal, which indicates that ancient Christians shared all things in common, is not entirely new.[6] The Lukan account of Acts testifies to a sharing of communal property in some sense, and the Apostle Paul later writes about an equalizing taking place between giver and recipient (2 Corinthians 8:13–15), an idea that he finds supported in the Hebrew Bible (Exodus 16:18). Paul's advocacy for equalizing material goods ultimately occurs within the context of a letter addressed to Corinthian Christians (cf. Romans 15:25–27; 1 Corinthians 16:1–4). In

5. Ward, *The Case for Religion*, 66.
6. See Crawford, *What Is Religion?*, 165.

this particular correspondence, the author exhorts his readers to support a ministry for poor Christians; moreover, one encounters similar ideas in the Qumran scrolls of the Dead Sea Community. Tertullian (ca. 160–240 C.E.), a North African apologist belonging to the church, likewise refers to the ecclesiastical practice of holding material goods in common (Apology 39.11). Still, Montero's study is unique insofar as he argues that early Christians lived by the communitarian principle, they shared all things in common, and the early followers of Jesus subsequently thrived—even outlasting the indomitable Roman Empire that persecuted the nascent ecclesia, sometimes quite brutally.

Montero suggests that the practices outlined by Luke were not limited to a few congregations or to a circumscribed area. To the contrary, he thinks early followers of Jesus applied "*From each according to his ability, to each according to his needs*" across the entire Greco-Roman world for at least the first two centuries of the Christian community's existence. If his idea turns out to fit the evidence, then a case would be made that when this principle is applied within a Christian setting or implemented properly, then it possibly might yield a unified and budding community that honors God. Nevertheless, how does one go about examining such an idea? Which scholarly methods should be utilized?

The current study invokes historical, economic, and sociological evidence while refusing to ignore Scriptural or theological factors. The methodology is varied: Jewish texts are examined; so are Christian and Greco-Roman sources. Economic practices receive the primary emphasis, but they are coupled with historical analyses of primary sources and the study demonstrates adequate sensitivity for sociocultural context. Whatever one might think of Marxism and its possible relationship with the early Christian community, students of the social sciences and Scripture will find Montero's study to be refreshing, objective, and a genuine contribution to our knowledge of ecclesiastical history. He also goes beyond theoretical considerations in order to show the practical relevance of the texts from Acts and the author's intriguing suggestion posits that the early communal practices outlined by Luke ultimately originated with Jesus of Nazareth. The main arguments in this book, while provocative, admittedly run counter to the contemporary promotion of laissez-faire capitalism. But that has been the longstanding conflict between Scripture and modern-day capitalism. Regardless of which economic theory that one espouses, there is much to be learned from a new examination of ancient economics undertaken through the prism of early Christianity.

Edgar G. Foster
Lenoir-Rhyne University
January 2017

Introduction

> In a higher phase of communist society, . . .—only then can the
> narrow horizon of bourgeois right be crossed in its entirety and
> society inscribe on its banners: From each according to his ability,
> to each according to his needs![1]

THIS WAS WRITTEN IN 1875 by Karl Marx in his *Critique of the Gotha Program*. The phrase was used within the socialist movement prior to Marx,
but his usage made the phrase famous and almost universally recognizable.
Coming out of the enlightenment era, the idea of socialism and communism took liberal enlightenment principles and expanded on them—add-
ing to them the dream of a truly egalitarian and universal society where the
principle "from each according to his ability to each according to his need"
could be implemented.

On one level, this principle seems almost instinctually self-evident.
Why would we not run things according to that principle? It seems like
things would be so pleasant if people gave all they could and took only what
they needed. Yet on the other hand it seems so detached from the reality
and brutality of the modern world. We look around and see a world run by
the relentless pursuit of individual profit; and masses of people who are left
to fight for the scraps.

Since the twentieth century, various movements have tried to move
on these principles, attempting to overcome the alienation and exploitation of capitalism through reform or revolution. From Marxist-Leninists
to European social democrats to third-world revolutionaries to Anarchists,

---

1. Marx, *Critique of the Gotha Program*, 17.

many such movements have risen and fallen. The most famous and extreme of these movements resulted in some of the most barbaric and murderous regimes of history: the Stalinist Soviet Union and Maoist China. Other segments of these movements have left a lasting mark on capitalism itself: leaving behind things like workers' rights, social welfare programs, public services, labor unions, cooperatives, concepts of economic solidarity, and so on.

Nevertheless, there are many who look at the principle "from each according to his ability, to each according to his need" with disdain. They view anything deviating from the Lockean/Adam Smith principles of absolute private property, self-interest, market exchange, and profit seeking as a recipe for disaster; and regard any dream of an egalitarian society as a dangerous pipe dream. For these individuals, society is nothing more than a system of markets; capitalism is the basic way society functions, and it is here to stay—any deviation from it is destined to end up in failure.

This dream—the dream of a society that follows the principle "from each according to his ability, to each according to his need," a society based on economic egalitarianism and solidarity still captures the hearts and minds of millions worldwide. There is something in this idea that still captivates many, if only as an exciting fantasy; philosopher Alain Badiou puts it this way:

> And that is one of the Idea's [the idea of communism that is] functions: to project the exception into the ordinary life of individuals, to fill what merely exists with a certain measure of the extraordinary. To convince my own immediate circle—husband or wife, neighbours and friends, colleagues—that the fantastic exception of truths in the making also exists, that we are not doomed to lives programmed by the constraints of the State[the capitalist state].[2]

Yet for many, the idea of a society based on the principle "from each according to his ability and to each according to his need" seems like a pie in the sky; for many, the best one could hope for is a mere softening of the negative effects of capitalism. It seems to some that human selfishness and greed simply cannot allow for such a society to exist, and that the horrors of the Leninist states and the prospect of the dismantling of the social democracies of Europe appear to attest to that sentiment.

Centuries before Karl Marx was even born, in the first century C.E. this principle was written about, not as an idea for which one should fight,

2. Badiou, *The Communist Hypothesis*, 253.

not as a future utopian society; but rather as a description of an actually existing community. I am referring to chapters 2 and 4 of the Acts of the Apostles, both of which contain a description of the early Christian community:

> All who believed were together and had all things in common; they would sell their possessions and goods and distribute the proceeds to all, as any had need . . . (Acts 2:44–45)

> . . .

> Now the whole group of those who believed were of one heart and soul, and no one claimed private ownership of any possessions, but everything they owned was held in common. With great power the apostles gave their testimony to the resurrection of the Lord Jesus, and great grace was upon them all. There was not a needy person among them, for as many as owned lands or houses sold them and brought the proceeds of what was sold. They laid it at the apostles' feet, and it was distributed to each as any had need. (Acts 4:32–35)

Anyone interested in early Christian history, Christian theology and ethics, or the history of egalitarian economic thought and practice, should be interested in these two passages. If it is the case that centuries before the enlightenment, centuries before the birth of liberalism, democracy, and socialism, there existed a community—which was not based on ethnicity but which functioned on explicitly egalitarian principles; not as a tribal or primitive communist society, but rather as an intentional community following ideological principles, within the context of a brutal and oppressive society such as the Roman Empire—then we should conclude that the Enlightenment was not the birth of the ideals of egalitarianism and universalism: rather, it was Christianity. What others merely dream about—actually was a reality in what Acts describes.

If it is true that, in the middle of one of the most brutal and totalizing empires of history, a small group created a community based on solidarity, a community that not only existed but flourished; eventually conquering the most powerful empire the world had ever seen through word rather than sword—then any subsequent attempt to revolutionize society in order to build a community based on solidarity and equality is really just an imitation.

Individualistic market ideology has infiltrated almost all aspects of modern life, there seems to be almost no realm left that capitalism has not yet engulfed. Growing up in this kind of world leaves us with an imaginative handicap: we tend to think of everything as a commodity, everyone as either an entrepreneur or a consumer, and every relationship as a market exchange. Even those who wish to break free from this ideological hegemony find it difficult to think outside of the categories of capitalism. But if we look back to history—specifically to what I contend is the greatest example of a community of solidarity based on the principle "from each according to his ability, to each according to his need;" a community that broke free from the dominant ideology of its time (the early Christian community that is)—we can expand our horizons, and see that there may be an alternative to the ruling ideologies; although it may not be what we expected.

For any who care about Christian ethics, these two passages ought to be of utmost importance; those who care about Christian ethics ought to try and understand why Luke was compelled to detail, twice, the communal practices of the early Christians and to consider what the ethical implications are for Christians today. For any who care about the history of Christianity, these two passages will give a window into the development of social relationships and the community of goods among Christians—distinct among the greater Roman world—which cries out for an explanation. If anyone cares about making the world a better place; undoing the alienation, exploitation, and nihilism of the modern capitalist world in order to attempt to build a society based on solidarity and community, it would behoove such one to study an example of a movement that accomplished just that.

My goal in the following chapters is to examine if those two passages describe historical practices, and if so what they were. I will examine what economic practices the early Christian community had, how they were practiced; as well as how widespread and long lasting these practices were.

In doing so, I am going to examine various early Christian texts, various Jewish texts, as well as Greco-Roman writings—which will shed light on the early Christian economic practices. I will do so through the framework of social relationships as employed by anthropologists to study communities; as opposed to political categories or categories taken from the field of economics. I claim that approaching the economic practices of the early Christians using an anthropological framework will allow us to make sense of the sources in a way that other frameworks—such as those of politics or modern economics—simply cannot.

I am going to argue that the accounts found in Acts 2:42–47 and Acts 4:32–37 describe historical economic practices found within the early Christian community; practices that were taken very seriously, which were widespread over different Christian communities around the Roman world, and which lasted for at least well into the second century. I am also going to argue that these economic practices were grounded in both Jewish and Christian theology and had precedent in Jewish tradition and practice; as well as the teachings of Jesus of Nazareth.

1

The Economic Context of First-Century Palestine

WE FIRST NEED TO examine the economic world in which the first Christian community[1] found itself. Given that, according to Acts, the first Christian communities were found in Palestine; we will limit our examination to that region. Christianity very soon spread throughout the Roman world, but the economic practices in which we are interested are described as having started in Palestine; therefore first-century Palestine is the most relevant context for examining the birth of Christianity along with its practices. Palestine in the first century was a society in which the class in which one was born would determine almost everything about one's life.

The vast majority of the population were desperately poor, living near or at a sustenance level, with a few people living at a level which we would today, rather anachronistically, call "middle class" (merchants, small businessmen, and so on), and even fewer elites. There was a strong distinction between the city and the countryside: the former being where the elites lived along with the urban poor, and the latter being where the majority of the population lived as peasants. When we talk about the poverty of this time, we are talking about devastating and extreme poverty, where people would often go hungry. In the book *Christian Origins: a People's History of Christianity*, Warren Carter writes:

---

1. The term "Christian" cannot be applied to the earliest followers of Jesus since the term was first used in Antioch (Acts 11:26) to apply to followers of Jesus, but for the sake of clarity I will be using the term "Christian" to refer to the followers of Jesus.

Food shortages were frequent as a result of bad harvests, unfavorable weather, distribution difficulties, speculation by traders (see Philostratus, Life of Apollonius 1.8), wars, taxes, and so forth. Shortages meant endemic undernourishment or chronic malnutrition, especially for the poor.[2]

By modern standards, we would say that life was extremely hard and brutal for the vast majority of the population. In this kind of environment, getting enough food for the day was not something guaranteed; and having access to sources of food and shelter would be, for many, a daily matter of life and death. Dominating over the population were the institutions of political, religious, and economic power. The most powerful economic institutions in Palestine were the Roman state—which ruled through its local representatives and officials, the Herodian elite, and the temple—along with the leading priests. These three institutions worked in concert with, and depended upon one another for their political and economic power. The Roman state kept the Herodian elite in power; the Herodian elite appointed and supported the temple leadership; the temple leadership received benefits and sanction from the Roman State; the Herodian elite ruled on behalf of the Roman state and enforced its sovereignty; and the temple legitimated both the Herodian elite and Roman rule.

The Roman state ruled primarily through military power which facilitated the collecting of taxes and tributes. The Herodian elite ruled primarily through taxation, the ownership of land, and the collection of land rents; and the temple elite ran financial institutions, owned vast amounts of land, and received temple taxes. All of the power elites ruled through economic power—property and rents—which was backed up by the sword.

The Herodian elite, for much of the first century C.E., were the aristocracy of Judea and Galilee; Herodian through their loyalty to the Herodian dynasty and its policies, and aristocratic through birth and landownership. These individuals would have been the direct political and economic power in Palestine, and were representations of Roman power and domination to the common people. The Herodians had to constantly ride a thin line between respecting the Judean customs and religion, and keeping the Roman peace and maintaining economic and political power (which, as we will see later, could often be in conflict). When we talk of maintaining the Roman peace, what we really mean is securing the tribute to Rome—not only for the sake of Rome but also for the Herodian's pockets—since the Herodian

2. Carter, "Matthew's People," 156–157.

dynasty depended on Rome for its hegemony, and the Herodian aristo-cratic families depended on the dynasty's survival for their own wealth.[3] They needed the support of the temple in order to gain legitimacy from the Jewish people, and they needed the support of Rome for the muscle to protect their power.

Of the actual economic institutions through which economic power was wielded, the temple in Jerusalem, along with its priesthood, was one of the most important and wealthy. This institution was also largely controlled by Herod, through his appointments of various High Priests—appoint-ments made for almost entirely political purposes.[4] After Herod's death, appointments were made by whomever happened to be ruling Jerusalem, and these appointments were also very often politically motivated.

The priesthood in Judah was extremely wealthy; holding the best lands, and gaining large amounts of wealth through constant taxes, land rents, and the receiving of offerings. This was the case despite the biblical mandate that the Levite priesthood ought not to hold land; a fact that tells us that many in the priesthood were probably slightly more mercenary in their vocation than they were pious.[5] The temple employed a vast number of lay workers, doing various types of work related to the running of the temple and its economic interests. Either indirectly or directly, a huge portion of the population of Jerusalem relied on the temple for their income; either by directly working for the temple priesthood or working in industries that supplied and supported the temple establishment. You could say that the temple was itself an entire economy; but it was a top-down economy. The lay workers, despite their necessary function, were considered to be lower in status than the priesthood, and looked down on by the priesthood; often due to purity concerns and the fact that some of the trades done by the lay workers were considered to be undignified by the Jewish religious leaders.[6]

Looking at these two power groups, not to mention the all-powerful Roman state, we can imagine a symbiotic relationship of political, religious, and economic power; a power-triad which would seem almost unbreakable to the populous.

It is often pointed out that the economy grew significantly during the time of King Herod, and that a lot of wealth came to Judea and Galilee

---

3. Freyne, "Galilee and Judea in the first century," 43.
4. Josephus, *Antiquities*, 15.2.4; 15.3.1; 15.3.3; 15.9.3; 17.4.2; 17.6.4.
5. Freyne, "Galilee and Judea in the first century," 50.
6. Freyne, "Galilee and Judea in the first century," 49–50.

during that period. This was in no small part due to the fact that King Herod started many large building projects,[7] and even enacted some welfare policies during a famine.[8] These building projects (which included Herod's great expansion of the temple) no doubt jump-started the economy, employing many artisans and increasing revenue and employment from trade. However, there was, as there almost always is, a flip side to the economic growth. In the book *Christian Origins: a People's history of Christianity*, William Herzog writes:

> While the extent of tribute and taxation is debated, most estimates run between 25 and 30 percent of a peasant's harvest.
>
> . . .
>
> Taxes were no doubt increased to support these building projects (of Herod Antipas). And the close proximity of the ruling class to the villages meant that the peasants would have been subjected to an ever more efficient and intrusive collection of rents and indirect taxation. The peasants of Galilee thus came under increasing economic stress. Many were forced to borrow to plant their crops, a move that set them on a path that often led to the loss of land through the use of debt instruments.[9]

Richard Horsley in the same work writes:

> With peasant families forced into escalating debt in order to pay taxes and still support themselves, village communities were threatened with disintegration.[10]

These building projects were paid for by taxation and land rents, and many peasants fell deeply into debt; many of those lost their land due to foreclosure—their land almost always ending up in the hands of the Herodian aristocrats, or wealthy priests.[11] After Herod the Great died, the kingdom was split up and Herod Antipas ruled over Galilee (where Jesus was from); whereas Judea was left to Herod Archelaus, but soon after became a Roman province ruled directly by a Roman procurator. Herod Antipas

---

7. Josephus, *Antiquities,* 15.11; 16.5.

8. Josephus, *Antiquities,* 15.9.

9. Herzog, "Why Peasants Responded to Jesus," 50.

10. Horsley, "Jesus Movements and the Renewal of Israel," 35.

11. Horsley, "Jesus Movements and the Renewal of Israel," 35.

in Galilee continued the policy of expansion and growth; this continued expansion pulled even more resources from the countryside and villages into the cities, it also increased taxation and thus increased the demand for money; which in turn increased debt (sustenance farmers often lived off what they and their neighbors grew, and only sold a small surplus; therefore an increase of taxation would often require the borrowing of money). This meant that larger wealthier estates could take control of more land which poorer families could not maintain (due to increasing taxation and rent burdens), or which had been foreclosed on. These factors exacerbated the social divide between city and countryside, rich and poor.[12] Judea under the procurators fared no better; Philo describes the procurator Pontius Pilate (under whom Jesus was killed) as being guilty:

> in respect of his corruption, and his acts of insolence, and his rapine, and his habit of insulting people, and his cruelty, and his continual murders of people untried and uncondemned, and his never ending, and gratuitous, and most grievous inhumanity. (Philo, *Embassy to Gaius*, 18.302 [Yong])

In Palestine, the first half of the first century was a time of great economic growth with some people growing extremely wealthy; while others were either barely holding on, or falling into desperate poverty under despotic rulers who ruled on behalf of the Roman state.

Like many modern economies—where there is vast economic growth in which the distribution is heavily tilted toward the urban rich—many of the poor in first-century Palestine, especially the rural poor, got the short end of the stick. The growth of urbanization meant that peasants would fall deeper into debt as taxation burdens became too high and eventually lose their lands; forcing them to the city to work as wage laborers. Peasants who did not lose their lands would still often have to work as wage laborers in the city to supplement their income.[13] These changes would bring with them social alienation, as workers were separated from their families and their traditional village economies. These changes would also increase desperation among these wage laborers when the urban growth slowed down and wage laborers turned into precarious workers or became unemployed, still without any land.

---

12. Meyes and Chancey, *Alexander to Constantine*, 120.
13. Horsley, "Jesus Movements and the Renewal of Israel," 35.

The corrupt and well-connected elite gained a steady stream of wealth through rents and taxes, while the poor suffered and were abused, their livelihoods always resting on a knife's edge. Many of the parables of Jesus reflect these conditions in their dealing with debt, class relations, and wealth and poverty.[14] The use of these parables by Jesus gives us a window into what the concerns of the Palestinian poor were. Things like debt, wages, harvests, debt collection, economic ruin, hunger, and so on were all things that permeated Jesus's teachings, and things that were clearly on the minds of anxious Galilean and Judean peasants and workers.

The average peasant in Palestine during this period would have been under constant risk of becoming destitute. As land rents rose, incomes would have had to also rise; if they did not rise, the peasant would have to supplement his income somehow. If he could not make his rent he risked being removed from his land and perhaps having to go to the city to earn a wage for his survival. If he could not do that—perhaps the work was simply not available—he may end up as a beggar. His life and the lives of those in his family who depended on him were constantly at risk. At the same time this peasant would see major growth in the cities; villas being built, wealth being accumulated (just not by him or his neighbors), and his Jewish culture being compromised through Greco-Roman influence.

Such social conditions were ripe for unrest, and there certainly was plenty of social unrest during that time. Around 6 C.E. the Romans conducted a census of Palestine for the purpose of taxation; and in response, a popular rebellion arose led by a Judas of Galilee. The rebellion was based on the idea that submitting to the census was no better than slavery; this rebellion in hindsight (at least in the eyes of Josephus) was the beginning of a great deal of civil strife to come.[15] There were riots, messianic movements and their consequent repression, building up to the full-fledged rebellion in 66 C.E.—described by Josephus in *the War of the Jews*—ending up with the destruction of Jerusalem and her temple.

One of the very first actions of the Jewish revolutionaries (Zealots and Sacarii) during the First Jewish-Roman war, starting in 66 C.E., was to destroy the debt records. They did so, according to Josephus, to convince the

14. For example: Luke 7:41–43; 12:16–21; 16:1–12; 19–31; 19:12–17; Matthew 20:1–16; 25:24–30.

15. Josephus, *Antiquities,* 18.1.1.

poor to join their rebellion—specifically against the wealthy and powerful, and ultimately against the Romans.[16]

We can understand from this act that the major economic issue of the poor was debt, along with imperial taxation, which led to dispossession. It was such an important issue, at least at the time of the First Jewish-Roman war, that the destruction of debt records was enough to convince many of the poor to risk their lives in rebellion. Clearly debt was seen as a major source of oppression by much of the Judean and Galilean population. The differences between the ruling class and the poor were huge, and they were just getting worse with time. Palestine was densely populated and the aristocracy was growing in wealth by taking more and more of the limited land supply. The poor were holding on to what they had if they were lucky, but many were sliding down the social ladder.[17] Resentment and anger was growing and something needed to be done about it; the Zealots and Sacarii of the First Jewish-Roman war viewed revolution as the solution.

The economic, religious, and political spheres in first-century Palestine were inseparable; the temple was religious in nature as well as economic and political. The Herodian elite were legitimated through Rome and appointed the high priesthood, which in turn sanctioned the Herodian elite; and were thus legitimated religiously and politically. Naturally, the oppositions to the ruling classes were also often religious, political, and economic at the same time. For example; the Zealots wanted to restore true Judaism, they wanted political independence, and they sought justice for the poor. These three goals were inseparable in the minds of the Zealots.

The Jewish tradition was not economically neutral; there was found within it an ideal of abundance for everyone, a shared prosperity, and primary attention given to the poor. Against the reality of the Palestinian ruling classes siphoning more and more wealth for themselves, and the poor being left with less and less, stood an enduring ideal of abundance for everyone, shared prosperity, primary attention to the poor, and an ideal of the community sharing the land.[18] This tradition included regulations in the Torah; such as the gleaning laws, the Sabbatical and Jubilee laws, the anti-usury laws, and the constant reminders to put the interests of the poor first.[19] It

16. Josephus, *War*, 2.17.6.

17. Freyne, "Galilee and Judea in the first century," 44.

18. Freyne, "Galilee and Judea in the first century," 47.

19. For example: Exodus 22:22–27; 23:10–11; Leviticus 19:9–10; 23:22; 25:1–55; Deuteronomy 15:1–18; 24:10–21.

included the prophetic tradition, which constantly spoke on behalf of the poor and against the oppressor.[20] There was also the wisdom literature and psalms, which had within them models for righteous government.[21]

The prophetic traditions also held within them promises of a messianic age, the idea of Israel being blessed, motifs of liberation and shared blessings; and yet the reality was so different. From this dichotomy came the constant unrest, rebellion, and liberation movements that we find in first-century Palestine. Not only was the reality completely different from the biblical ideal, but also the ones who should have been faithful to the biblical ideal, the priesthood and the kings, were the ones who were leading the unjust treatment of the poor—causing their suffering. The priesthood also enabled Roman hegemony and the abandonment of Jewish piety.

The world in which Christianity began was one of messianic idealism on the one hand; and brutal poverty, oppression, and corruption on the other hand. It was a world in which the major source of wealth, land, was almost entirely moving into the hands of the ruling class, and more and more peasants were being reduced to wage laborers and debt slaves.

That being said, there was a socio-religious culture of social welfare within the Jewish world. Poverty in the Jewish tradition was not idealized, it was recognized as something harsh and brutal; and the tradition put a large responsibility on the community to care for the poor—from Torah legislation to prophetic denunciations and pleading.[22] This differed from the Hellenistic and Roman attitude towards the poor; in those cultures, things like mercy and pity were not considered virtues at all. The Greco-Roman attitude was that mercy and pity were based on emotion, not reason—and the ideal was to be a man driven by reason, not swayed back and forth by weak impulses like pity. They also held that mercy, by definition, was unearned and thus contrary to justice.[23]

When we consider the birth of the Christian movement, it is important to remember this background in order to understand how events would be interpreted and how people would respond to the Christian message. It is also important to understand the background in order to fully appreciate just how different the Christian community was from the society it came

---

20. For example: Isaiah 3:13–26; 10:1–4; 11:1–9; 41:17–29; 58:6–9; Amos 2:6–8; 4:1–5; 5:10–13; 8:4–15; Ezekiel 22:28–29.

21. For example: Psalm 72:1–20; Ecclesiastes 5:8–9; Sirach 4:1–10; 29:1–13; 35:14–26.

22. Dunn, *Christianity in the Making Vol. 1*, 510.

23. Stark, *The Triumph of Christianity*, 112.

from. The world in which Christianity grew was one in which brutal class oppression and dispossession happened at an alarmingly increasing rate, at the same time when ideas of shared prosperity from the Hebrew traditions and scriptures were brewing in the background.

The ground was fertile for change, for a messianic movement to challenge the powers, ideologies, and structures of that age.

2

Economic Relationships

SINCE WHAT WE ARE discussing is a kind of economic relationship or institution within the early Christian community, it would be helpful to define our terms. I use the term "economic relationship",[1] as opposed to "economic system", because "economic relationship" includes both formal and informal relationships; and because it sidesteps political connotations—most of which come from modern understandings of politics and economics, and which are not relevant to the subject at hand. In fact the very notion of "the economy", or an "economic system", is a modern construct and does not translate back well to the ancient world. The idea of an economic system really comes with the rise of modern science, and its drive to reduce everything to mathematically modelled systems—the field of economics and the concept of an economic system is an attempt to do that with human society itself. Therefore—in talking about the early Christians—we will instead talk about "economic relationships".[2]

1. The Term "social relationship" is used by anthropologists rather than "economic relationship" in describing the kind of social model described in this chapter. For the purpose of this book, however, I have in many places chosen to use "economic relationship" instead of "social relationship" because I will be applying the kind of social models described in this chapter mostly to questions concerning the distribution of goods and services among the participants, rather than things like sexual relationships, political relationships, or other areas of the human experience this kind of model can be applied to. When I use the term "social relationship" I am using it to refer to a more broad kind of relationship rather than the more specific application to the distribution of goods and services implied by the term "economic relationship".

2. Taylor, *A Secular Age,* 181.

In order to define what I mean by "economic relationship", I will present Alan Fiske's description of the kind of model I am using:

> Simply, every social relationship entails moral obligations, and every moral obligation derives from the imputation of a social relationship.[3]

What we are describing here are social norms of how individuals act, which have at their base moral obligations, and which are derived from the type of relationship those individuals have with one another. Examples of these moral obligations might be the obligation to respect property lines, the obligation to care for your child, the obligation to help an old lady cross the street, the obligation to answer a police officer, and so on and so forth.

Anthropologists have different ways of categorizing different types of economic relationships. I find David Graeber's discussion and categorization of these relationships most interesting and compelling, and it is his categorization that I will use going forward. Graeber describes three different moral principles on which economic relationships may be founded; those are hierarchy, exchange, and communism.[4] These principles are all found to varying degrees in every society; and different relationships, communities, and institutions enact them in different ways. On relations of explicit hierarchy, Graeber writes:

> That is, relations between at least two parties in which one is considered superior to the other—do not tend to operate by reciprocity at all. It's hard to see because the relation is often justified in reciprocal terms ("the peasants provide food, the lords provide protection"), but the principle by which they operate is exactly the opposite. In practice, hierarchy tends to work by a logic of precedent.[5]

An obvious example of this is the Roman state's right to collect taxes and the Judean peasant's obligation to pay those taxes. The former is clearly superior and the latter is clearly subject; the former is really in the business of wealth extraction by force, but justifies the practice by claiming it is bringing peace and security to the land (the Pax Romana). Another example of this kind of relationship is the patron-client relationship, which we will discuss later. A modern example would be an employer and an

---

3. Fiske, *Structures of Social Life,* 170.

4. Graeber, *Debt,* 94.

5. Graeber, *Debt,* 109.

employee: the latter is considered subject to the former and must obey (to a degree) the commands of the latter within the context of the workplace. This sort of social relationship is generally immediately recognizable, and it is found to varying degrees in all societies at all times. It is very clear cut: people know who is in charge and who is subject. This is especially the case if you happened to be the subject.

Exchange, Graeber writes:

> is all about equivalence. It's a back-and-forth process involving two sides in which each side gives as good as it gets. This is why one can speak of people exchanging words (if there is an argument), blows, or even gunfire. In these examples, it is not that there is ever an exact equivalence—even if there were some way to measure an exact equivalence—but more a constant process of interaction tending toward equivalence.[6]

Examples of this kind of relationship are also very easy to find. In fact, this moral principle is the ground and guiding principle of capitalism (just as hierarchy was the ground and guiding principle of feudalism). This is the kind of relationship underlying purchases, payment for services, or any kind of trade or market activity. The exchange relationship differs from hierarchy in that each party is considered to be roughly equal and autonomous, and only related to each other contingently in a contractual manner. One aspect of exchange that makes it unique is that it is completely impersonal and temporary. In an exchange relationship, especially a market exchange relationship, it is not at all important whom the exchange is with, and once the exchange is over, the relationship is over. Exchange relationships are, almost by definition, impersonal—which is one reason that doing business with a friend can be damaging to the friendship: exchange relationships are for strangers who wish to remain strangers, not for friends.[7]

Lastly, but not least, there is communism, about which Graeber writes:

> I will define communism here as any human relationship that operates on the principles of "from each according to their abilities, to each according to their needs."[8]

. . .

6. Graeber, *Debt*, 103.

7. Graeber, *Debt*, 103.

8. Graeber, *Debt*, 94.

Starting, as I say, from the principle of "from each according to their abilities, to each according to their needs" allows us to look past the question of individual or private ownership (which is often little more than formal legality anyway) and at much more immediate and practical questions of who has access to what sorts of things and under what conditions. Whenever it is the operative principle, even if it's just two people who are interacting, we can say we are in the presence of a sort of communism.[9]

The word "communism" can elicit a certain response due to the history of the twentieth century and the word's usage to describe a political system, ideology, or goal. This is not the "communism" we are talking about here. What we are talking about—following Graeber—is a moral principle which guides various kinds of relationships: from a group of friends working on a project together, to the common and basic expectation that a stranger would help another stranger in various circumstances, to a cooperative farm. The kind of communism we are talking about is any inter-personal relationship that functions on the basis of "from each according to his ability, to each according to his need," no matter where it is found and no matter its size or scope.

Unlike hierarchy and exchange; communism, at least in principle, renders questions of status verses equality irrelevant. In communism each person is simply expected to do his or her part and to only take what he or she needs—no comparison of status is necessary. This principle is extremely common; for example, when a smoker asks for a cigarette outside of a restaurant, it is considered good manners to hand over a cigarette if you have a spare one; if you are asking for a cigarette it would be considered rude to ask for more than what you are going to smoke right then and there. This scenario, of smokers outside of a restaurant, is a perfect example of communism: from each according to his ability (whatever cigarettes you have to spare) to each according to his need (only ask for whatever you are going to smoke right then and there).

Another unique aspect of communism is that, unlike hierarchy or exchange, there is an assumption of non-violence. Exchange and the use of bullion money, historically, predominated during periods of violence—this would make perfect sense if you think of the one quality that is more or less needed for a "communist" relationship—trust. For communism to work there has to be a level of trust that each person involved is going to

9. Graeber, *Debt*, 95.

participate in the relationship, taking only what he needs and giving what he can; if however, one of the parties displays a willingness to use violence to get his way, it becomes much more difficult to establish this trust. The less violence in a society, the more natural communist relationships are; the more violent the society, the more difficult they are.

Therefore, if there is a clear willingness to resort to violence, communism cannot work, so the parties must resort to something else. In exchange all you need to trust is your ability to calculate accurately, there is no need to trust any one individual, or any common morality—thus exchange works quite well for periods of violence.[10] Hierarchy is also related to violence in that it generally is the result of systematic violence that becomes framed and institutionalized in a moral code. A very clear example of this is the typical organized crime protection racket, or the mediaeval feudal system; the lord may like to frame the relationship in terms of honor or the natural order—but the real situation is generally just a case of the lord having the weapons and not the peasants.[11]

Outside of the possibility of violence, communism tends to be the basic way humans relate to each other; probably because it is simply the most efficient, easiest, and most pleasant way to get things done. If communism can be established one can avoid all the trouble of calculating costs and bartering, or constantly trying to maintain hierarchies—and instead simply get things done. Even in societies where violence is a reality, there still tends to be what David Graeber calls "baseline communism": a basic understanding that if the need is great enough, or the cost is reasonable enough—then the principle of communism would apply.[12]

In a society without money, or the threat of violence—barter would not be efficient at all, due to the problem of the "double coincidence of wants." To illustrate the problem; imagine a stateless (and therefore moneyless) community where Bob raises chickens and Tim has cows. Let us say that Bob needs some milk from Tim's cows; he could try and barter with Tim—offering Tim some eggs—but there is no guarantee that Tim wants some eggs, nor is there any guarantee that he really wants anything at all right now. Bob could go around town and find someone who happens to have milk, and also happens to want eggs; but there is no telling how long that will take. In this situation, what almost always actually ends up

10. Graeber, *Debt*, 213.

11. Graeber, *Debt*, 110.

12. Graeber, *Debt*, 98.

happening, is that Tim finds out that Bob wants some milk—and then gives him some milk; knowing that if he ever needed some eggs, Bob would almost definitely give him some eggs. Even if he does not need eggs any time soon, he knows that if he does need something, or needs help with something; people in the community will help him—knowing that he is a trust worthy guy who helps people out. Rather than barter, stateless communities tend to function on the basis of a network of assumed mutual obligations.[13] Barter, in a stateless community, will come into play if Bob just takes what he wants through force (or shows a willingness to do so)—in that situation Tim is likely to demand some exact equivalence in return.[14] Barter will also come into play if a state exists and demands taxation in the form of money (which the state itself creates); and thus creates a situation where everyone in the community has at least one constant need in common: money.[15]

Notice that the economic relationships we are talking about are not dealing with questions of property, nor are we dealing with legal matters around production and distribution. Those issues are more questions of legal codes and institutions that can have their moral basis in any of the three kinds of relationships. All three of these different kinds of economic relationships can be found in capitalist societies, socialist societies, feudal societies, primitive societies, and everything in between. Questions about property only exist in societies in which property rights are established as an institution (which has not been the case for all societies in history). Questions about how people relate to each other materially are universal, making them more pertinent to looking at economic relationships among non-state communities such as the early Christians.

That being said, the importance and place of property does change depending on the type of economic relationship emphasized within a given realm. For example who owns what will matter a whole lot more in a market place where exchange is emphasized than it will in a party among friends where communism is emphasized. To give an example, if I grab a beer out of the refrigerator at a market place and start drinking it, the response would probably be quite different than if I had done the same at a party among friends. Hierarchical relationships can make property increasingly irrelevant if the superior party can dictate what is done with the property of the inferior party. Similarly, communist relationships can make property

13. Graeber, *Debt*, 34–37.
14. Graeber, *Debt*, 61–62.
15. Graeber, *Debt*, 49–50.

increasingly irrelevant, as mutual obligations push goods and services into the commons. If people can expect that you are going to give what you can to whoever needs something, and only take what you need; it will not matter all that much who owns what. Exchange relationships, on the other hand, generally make property increasingly important since distinct property lines are required to calculate the exchanges.

Communities, societies, and cultures differ and change with regard to which of these moral principles they value the most, or on which of these moral principles they ground their ideology. But all societies contain all three to varying degrees. Generally, they are more or less invisible and we do not think about them all that much. For example, most people do not find it strange that you have to pay a doctor to examine you (exchange), but will not have to pay someone who helps you when you fall off your bike on the street (communism); nor do we find it strange that a government can set laws determining what we can and cannot do (hierarchy). Very often, more than one of these principles exist within one economic relationship. For example, it is not strange that your boss can tell you what to do during the workday (hierarchy), but this is only because earlier you signed a labor contract (exchange). At your workplace there may be an expectation that everyone will do what he or she can to accomplish a common goal or finish a shared project (communism).[16]

Things get really interesting when one principle starts to take over an area once held by another principle. This is happening now with information. Various websites like Wikipedia more or less function on the principle of communism (open access and free), whereas encyclopedias of old functioned on the principle of exchange (customers buy an encyclopedia and the contributors are paid). Marriages used to be, in some cultures at least, based on hierarchy; whereas in many modern western societies they have moved more towards communism; or sadly, exchange (depending on the marriage). In Europe, large swaths of land used to be designated as "the commons" for use by everyone and anyone (communism), but later became enclosed, privatized, and entered the market (exchange). The examples are endless, but these shifts can sometimes be the seeds for sweeping changes of entire societies, cultures, and ideologies. Ultimately, in our discussion of the economic practices of the early Christians, it is such a shift that is most interesting and that cries out for explanation.

16. Graeber, *Debt*, 95–96.

Different economic relationships affect inter-personal relationships in different ways. For example, exchange relationships end at the point of exchange. Once I purchase a car, I need not have anything more to do with the salesman. Communist relationships tend to tie people together through mutual obligations; for example, if I buy a stranger a beer, it would be considered rude if he took the beer and did not talk to me, or at least acknowledge me. In fact, usually there is the expectation that the person who received the beer would be willing to do something for me at some time in the future; in a sense me buying him a beer ties him to me to a small degree.

One unique aspect of communist relationships is that they have the assumption of permanence: the assumption that the relationship will go on forever—or at least be applicable forever. This is why people are willing to give what they can and take only what they need, the assumption is that the individuals involved are socially bound together. This would explain why communism is more likely to have a larger scope in a family then among strangers in an airport—since you know you can rely on your family members for years into the future; whereas someone at the airport will be out of your life in just a few hours at the most. This is even the case when a specific instance of a communist relationship is expected to be temporary; so for example if I spend my time caring for an elderly widow next door, who I know will die soon—even though the relationship between me and the widow is temporary—the communist relationships making up the society I live in, which morally compels neighbors to take care of each other, is permanent. Another example is how one deals with one's parents or grandparents—the relationship tends to be treated as though it were permanent—even though we know it is not, and there is not any apparent benefit gained in treating it as though it were.[17] It almost seems as though there is something within us that expects relationships to be eternal; which—outside of conditions of violence—compels us to relate to each other within the communist framework.

When speaking of things like "mutual obligations", in the context of a discussion of communist relationships in the early Christian communities, we must be careful to not impose modern Enlightenment thinking on the ancient world. For example, distinctions between voluntary actions (such as gift giving) and involuntary obligations are rather modern concepts that we must be careful not to impose on the ancient world. Anthropologist Marcel Mauss gives us a good warning in his book *The Gift*:

17. Graeber, *Debt*, 100.

Likewise our civilizations, ever since the Semitic, Greek, and Roman civilizations, draw a strong distinction between obligations and services that are not given free, on the one hand, and gifts, on the other. Yet are not such distinctions fairly recent in the legal systems of our great civilizations? Have these not gone through a previous phase in which they did not display such a cold, calculating mentality? Have they not in fact practised these customs of the gift that is exchanged, in which persons and things merge? The analysis of a few features of Indo-European legal systems will allow us to demonstrate that they have, indeed, undergone this metamorphosis.[18]

This is important to keep in mind because the modern concepts of communism generally bring to mind a legal framework established by the government; and many contrast such a formal system with voluntary contracts of the market or voluntary cooperation. However, in many ancient societies the distinction between voluntary and involuntary were not all that clear. In fact, the very concept of freedom—as the choice to choose whatever one wants with no obligations—is a relatively new one. Modern society makes a sharp division between freedom and obligation, as though the two were in conflict; this division is largely driven by market ideology which treats people as though they were atomized autonomous individuals who only contract themselves into relationship—a view of the world that is clearly mythical; all one has to do is look around at real human relationships to see that this view is not realistic. It is only through the anonymity of market relationships that we can ignore the fact that we rely on other people for almost everything in our life; and thus we can think of our freedom as separate from our obligations—as though our freedom did not depend on other people, and other people's freedom did not depend on us. In other words, the modern market society allows us to pretend that one man's freedom is not another man's obligation.[19] An easy way to demonstrate this is to simply think of the food supply; how free could you be had it not been for the countless people, relationships, and institutions that are required for you to put food on your table.

The concepts of freedom in ancient societies were saturated with obligations and value judgments; for the ancients freedom was inseparable from one's nature and what that nature dictated; for human beings this meant

18. Mauss, *The Gift*, 61.

19. Greaber, *Anthropological Theory of Value*, 220–221.

that freedom was meant to be the ability to realize your human essence.[20] The same disconnect arises when we talk about the modern distinctions between the civic sphere of politics and economics; and an absolute moral sphere—these distinctions are new and not at all universal. According to the philosopher Charles Taylor, pre-modern societies tended to conceive of themselves as embodying a metaphysical order, a chain of being; whereas modern societies tend to conceive of themselves as nothing more than the common actions which the individuals in that society carry out.[21] It is of vital importance that we do not impose these distinctions on the early Christian communities, their communities were not ones of autonomous agents choosing between options, nor was the society from which these communities arose. Rather, one's place in society and one's place in community was absolutely subject to moral laws; laws that were metaphysically prior to one's will.

Almost all of the language and conceptual frameworks we use to discuss economic relationships or economic ideologies today are completely determined by the modern ruling ideologies of capitalism and liberalism. In modern western society everything tends to be looked at from the viewpoint of market exchange; and thus in terms of property, cost and benefit, and profit; this is the case even though there is plenty of evidence that these notions are much less important in most societies than what the modern capitalist and liberal framework assumes.[22] This is especially true when we examine ancient communities. When looking at the early Christians we have to shed that modern framework and attempt to look at things from a fresh perspective.

When talking about the economic relationships and practices of the early Christian community, thinking in terms of more broad moral principles (such as Graeber's categories of hierarchy, exchange, and communism) will help us to avoid applying modern, post-Enlightenment concepts and categories where they are not warranted.

Just to take an obvious example of how using modern concepts and categories can go wrong when talking about ancient history, let us again look at the Zealot uprising in the 60s in Judea and Galilee.

The Zealots were in one sense what modern observers might consider left wing: they were extremely popular with the poor, opposed to the

20. Hart, *Atheist Delusions*, 24.

21. Taylor, *A Secular Age*, 192.

22. Fiske, "The Four Elementary Forms of Sociality," 707.

wealthy and powerful, and their political program included the redistribution of wealth from the rich to the poor.[23] They were also insistent on notions of liberty and liberation.[24] On the other hand however, they were what many today would call right wing: they were religious fundamentalists, fanatics, ethnic nationalists, and absolutists. If someone studying the Zealots attempted to apply modern political categories to them, they would inevitably come out with an incorrect understanding of who the Zealots were.

In order to further clarify the framework of economic relationships that I will use in the following chapters, I want to make a distinction between two different kinds of communist relationships. (This distinction can be applied to other kinds of relationships as well, but for the purpose of this book let us focus on communistic relationships). I want to separate communist relationships into informal and formal communism. Formal communism can be described as a relationship or institution in which the communist principle of "from each according to his ability, to each according to his need" underlying the relationship is regulated by rules, an authority, or some kind of formal institution. Examples of this might be a monastery, in which the monks living there follow a series of set rules that are based on the communist principle (from each according to his ability, to each according to his need); or national unemployment insurance schemes, in which the principle of communism is put into a state program with legal backing. Another example might be a cooperative workplace or a sports team—in which each person has an assigned role and is expected to do whatever they can for the common goal, and use whatever resources they need to do so.

Informal communism is a lot more common. This kind of communism describes relationships that follow the communist principle without any official rules, authorities, or formal institutional arrangements. Examples would include friends buying each other drinks at a bar, or people working on a project together, or the above mentioned scenario of smokers outside a restaurant. It includes many modern households or neighborhood relationships in which cooperation and sharing happen simply on the basis of a general feeling of moral obligation towards one's neighbor or family member. Even capitalist workplaces, internally, generally function on a "from each according to his ability, to each according to his need" principle.

---

23. Josephus, *War*, 2.17.6.

24. Josephus, *Antiquities*, 18.1.1; 18.1.6.

People within an office do not trade office supplies internally since the assumption is that employees are not going to simply walk away in the middle of a project, but are rather dedicated to getting the job done—further evidence that communism is often the most efficient way to get things done.

Karl Marx declared that the specter of communism was haunting Europe, yet anthropologists such as Graeber and Mauss would say the specter already lurks in almost every aspect of society. In any situation where people are working together without the balancing of accounts or without an authoritarian structure, there lurks the specter of communism. At least informal communism.[25]

When reading about the early Christian community, we should think of the economic relationships both as frameworks for understanding real, on-the-ground materially consequential economic relationships between people and communities; and as moral frameworks that dictate the way one would think about other people, about their communities, and the mutual obligations between people in their communities. We should think of the economic relationships both as practice and as ideology. The two sides of the coin, ideology and practice, are always tied together in any relationship or community. For example, for money to function, we not only need banks, governments, printers, and accountants; we also need the ideology that creates trust in money and enforces its use. We need a culture that encourages people to treat money as if it were really an objective measure of value that really reflected a contribution to society and held some sort of social power beyond merely being a social invention. Economic relations depend on ideology, and (as Karl Marx pointed out) the reverse is often just as true.

The scope and extent of informal communism generally depends on the culture and institutions of a society. Things like manners, customs, family values, and so on, all determine the scope and extent of informal communism. In addition, actual institutions and laws contribute or take away from informal communism; for example, how people behave in public parks generally follows an informal communist principle and thus public parks can contribute to that moral framework.

When we look at the early Christian community, these economic relationship distinctions become vitally important for examining, not only the relationships themselves, but also the scope, extent, and ideological sources of these relationships.

25. Greaber, *Anthropological Theory of Value*, 227.

3

The Essenes, a Jewish Messianic Community

BEFORE WE TURN TO the early Christian communities, let us take a look at a first-century Jewish group with very similar characteristics: the Essenes. The Essenes are described primarily by Philo of Alexandria, Josephus, and some of the documents found among the Dead Sea Scrolls (The Dead Sea Scrolls are commonly ascribed to a sect of Essenes living in Qumran, a view I will assume in this book).[1]

The Essenes are described by Josephus as being made up of two different groups: one that marries and one that does not.[2] Both groups are described as living among non-Essene Jews in various cities and towns. They have a welfare system, which exists to aid people both inside and outside of the community. Josephus describes them as having a community of goods, to the point to where there is an appearance of economic equality. Stewards are put in place in order to take care of the common goods, which are administered in a communistic way, for use by everyone in the community.[3] The language used by Josephus in connection with the Essenes is almost literally a prototype of the communist moral maxim (from each according to his ability, to each according to his need).[4]

According to Josephus the community was very religious, dedicated to prayer, study, and to the taking of sacred meals.[5] The group was very

1. Ferguson, *Backgrounds of Early Christianity*, 522–523.
2. Josephus, *War*, 2.8.2–3.
3. Josephus, *War*, 2.8.3–4.
4. Josephus, *War*, 2.8.4.
5. Josephus, *War*, 2.8.5.

well organized and its membership was exclusive; with different ranks, and even a trial period required before one could join. They were also quite concerned with purity and rituals surrounding purity.[6]

When it comes to what the nature of the community of goods was, we run into somewhat of a problem in trying to reconstruct it. This problem can be demonstrated by looking at some passages describing the community of goods:

> Nor is there any one to be found among them who hath more than another; for it is a law among them, that those who come to them must let what they have be common to the whole order,—insomuch that among them all there is no appearance of poverty, or excess of riches, but every one's possessions are intermingled with every other's possessions; and so there is, as it were, one patrimony among all the brethren.
>
> . . .
>
> They also have stewards appointed to take care of their common affairs, who every one of them have no separate business for any, but what is for the uses of them all.
>
> . . .
>
> Nor do they either buy or sell anything to one another; but every one of them gives what he hath to him that wanteth it, and receives from him again in lieu of it what may be convenient for himself; and although there be no requital made, they are fully allowed to take what they want of whomsoever they please. (Josephus, *War*, 2.8 [Whiston])

The first two passages seem to contradict the last passage. How can Josephus say that what they have is common to the whole order and that they have all their possessions intermingled in the first two passages; yet at the same time say that all giving and receiving is voluntary in the third? If we take the statement that they have all things in common to mean that all property is literally common property, then it would make no sense for them to give and receive since everything is already common property. It would be kind of like me saying that I gave, as a gift, the coffee machine in my home to my wife; it would not make sense to give the coffee machine

6. Josephus, *War*, 2.8.10.

to her as a gift due to the fact that we already share the coffee machine in common at home. We have the same contradiction with the Essenes as described by Josephus: how can there be voluntary giving and receiving if everything is already common property. Before we address this apparent contradiction, let us look at Philo's descriptions of the Essenes and then at the Dead Sea scroll documents; then, once we have the larger picture, we can try to figure out what to make of this apparent contradiction.

Philo's descriptions are a little bit more fanciful and eccentric than Josephus's. He describes the Essenes as practicing a strict, literal kind of communism. He describes how individual Essenes would work as wage workers and then pool the money they earn together through a steward, who in turn distributes to the members according to their needs. Philo, like Josephus, describes a kind of welfare system; but Philo also includes details about how the wealth from the welfare system was used for the sick and elderly within the community.[7]

Another detail that Philo adds is that the Essenes seem to have been pacifists, or at least unwilling to produce instruments of war (although Josephus contradicts Philo in this regard, saying the Essenes carried weapons).[8] They also, according to Philo, eliminated slavery. The kind of communism described by Philo differs from Josephus in that it describes more clearly an absolute kind of communism: all things, down to even clothes and food, are shared commonly according to Philo. One of the groups Philo describes—differing from Josephus's description—stays away from cities, separates themselves from the outside world, and is numbered precisely four thousand.[9]

Both Josephus and Philo list two communities of Essenes (although they differ in what distinguishes the two communities), and both writers mention what seems to be a kind of literal communism, as well as a welfare system.

Moving on, let us look at the Dead Sea Scroll documents. The most relevant of the documents are the Community Rule, also known as the Manual of Discipline (1QS); and the Damascus Document, also known as the Covenant of Damascus (CD, 4Q265–73, 5Q12, 6Q15). These two documents are rather like rulebooks for their respective communities: two different rule books for two different communities of Essenes. That there

---

7. Eusebius, *Praeparatio Evangelica*, 8.11.

8. Josephus, *War*, 2.8.4.

9. Eusebius, *Praeparatio Evangelica*, 8.12.

are more than one type of community described in the Dead Sea Scroll documents fits with how both Josephus and Philo describe the Essenes.[10]

The Community Rule describes a community that lives in a kind of monastic way. It was a community that was both exclusive and insular: only accepting those who agree to live by strict rules, and excluding those who are not deemed to be pure enough.[11] The rulebook requires that one spend a year as a prospect before he could be admitted into the community—during which he would not have access to the common fund or be able to partake from sacred common meals. After the trial year, his property would be handed over to the community, but not yet made available for common use. He would then spend another year with the community—and after that year (two years in total) the community would vote on whether or not he should be a full member. If he is voted in, then he becomes a full member and has full access to the common property and can partake from the sacred common meals.[12]

The community described by the Community Rule seems to have held things in common in a literal and regulated way. This way of doing things would be considered to represent an example of formal communism using my own definition of that term (i.e., communism governed by clear rules and regulations). There were strict rules regarding property, and the leaders of the community had stewardship and authority over how the common property was administered,[13] this fits nicely into the category of formal communism.

The Damascus Document describes a community that was not nearly as insular or exclusive as the community of the Community Rule was. The Damascus Document describes groups that lived within camps as well as other groups that lived among the larger society (very much like the descriptions of the Essenes by Josephus and Philo). Unlike the community of the Community rule; the community of the Damascus Document seems to be made up of people who lived relatively normal lives: marrying and having families.[14] Unlike the Community Rule document, the Damascus Document assumes that individuals would hold a certain amount of private property; which we know based on the fact that there are guidelines on

10. Meyes and Chancey, *Alexander to Constantine,* 92.

11. 1QS, 1–2;5.

12. 1QS, 6.

13. 1QS, 1.

14. CD, 6–7.

property disputes and procedures on what to do with lost property.[15] But there was also a system of formal communism in place that consisted of a monthly tax that amounted to two days' worth of wages that was levied by the "guardian" of the community and the judges on behalf of the needy among them: the sick, the elderly, the orphans, widows, people without families, people taken captive in a foreign land, and the poor in general.[16] However, even when it came to private property and private dealings, one would have to inform the "guardian" of the community before engaging in commercial activity; thus individual commercial activity was subjected to the interests of the common good.[17] The private property of the members of the community was not fully private in the sense that we would think of it today: it was partially private, in that other people did not have a right to just take it; and partially common, in that its use was regulated for the sake of the common good. This can also be described in some ways as a type of formal communism: submitting the use of private property to the higher principle of the common good through formal rules and authority structures.

The Damascus Document has a theme of caring for the poor, the needy, and strangers (very common in ancient Jewish literature)—which serves as a kind of enforcement of the moral framework necessary in order to create informal communistic relationships; this theme is linked within the document with the Levitical command to love one's neighbor as one's self.[18] This theme is not at all unique to the Qumran community (a sect of the Essenes, if the assumption that the Qumran community was an Essene sect is correct); it was widespread in first-century Judaism. But in these Essene groups, we see these principles put into practice systematically around the time of Jesus and his preaching.

These moral enforcements of informal communism, although not as cut and dry as the rules of formal communism, should nonetheless not be taken lightly or seen as less influential. It is very often the case that ethical concerns shape economic relationships in a much more concrete and stable manner than rules do; and it is generally the case that the ethical concerns are what shape the rules, and the rules are only as good as the ethical concerns they are based on. To illustrate, if I make a rule for my daughter that

15. CD, 9.
16. CD, 14.
17. CD, 13.
18. CD, 6–7.

she must share her toys and dictate how she must do so; she might share her toys a little bit, but perhaps just enough to satisfy the rule I laid down, and she might try to get out of sharing when she can. But if I do not make a rule, but rather tell her that I will be very proud of her if she shares her toys and very disappointed if she does not; the moral pressure and desire for approval from her father will likely be much more influential, and will likely shape the child's behavior much more than a straight forward rule would. Obeying a rule does not earn an individual moral praise, whereas obeying a moral principle does.

Let us now re-examine the apparent contradiction we saw in Josephus's description. The contradiction is this: How can the Essenes be compelled to surrender their property and have everything in common as a requirement of membership, having all their possessions intermingled; yet at the same time be giving and receiving goods voluntarily?

This is where the distinction between informal communism and formal communism becomes extremely helpful. It is quite clear that there were various groups of Essenes with different sets of rules, and that all of them practiced a degree of formal communism; either to a large extent (the "Community Rule" group and the Essenes as described by Philo), or to a smaller extent (the "Damascus Document" group). If, however, in the case of the Essenes as described by Josephus, we are seeing a description of both formal and informal communism at the same time—we no longer have a contradiction.

The formal communism part of the description would be the garnishing of wages, or taxation, for the sake of the needy—such as described in the Damascus Document. The informal communism part of the description would be the general moral principle of sharing, which was not enforced by formal rules, but rather by ethical instruction and moral obligation. This distinction would explain how they could both hold all things in common (in a formal sense with the welfare system, as well as in the sense of having a communist moral foundation of the community); while at the same time be freely giving of their property as they wish (which would describe the concrete informal communist relationships between members of the community, which were not dictated by rules or authority structures).

So the phrase "all things in common" could be describing a general moral framework of communism, as well as a way of organizing certain goods. But the general moral framework—which is the mechanism that leads to a situation where it can be said by Josephus that "all things are held in common"—works itself out through the free sharing of goods, and doing so voluntarily. (Voluntarily in the sense that there is no threat of force, not necessarily that the members of the community were morally free to ignore the moral principles if they so wished; once again, we should not read modern Enlightenment concepts of freedom into ancient documents).

We should therefore read "all things in common" not so much in the sense of property law or a description of the ownership of things; but rather as the real economic and social outcome of a moral framework along with the economic institutions that were built out of that moral framework.

What we can say from the sources about the Essenes is the following: There were various groups with a range of religious, social, and economic practices. There were some more isolated groups practicing a strict ascetic religious life and a very strict formal communism, and there were other groups that were not so isolated and that practiced a limited kind of formal communism while also practicing informal communism which was based on moral obligations. But they all could be described as holding "all things in common" as a result of their communist moral framework and their social welfare distributive systems—even though these frameworks and systems were worked out somewhat differently by different Essene groups.

Another aspect of the Essenes that is very important, for the sake of comparison with the early Christian communities, is the theological character of the group—especially as described in the Damascus Document. The opening of the Damascus document gives a history of the community: a kind of founding myth, as well as the community's eschatology. The general idea is more or less that Israel strays from righteousness and a remnant stays faithful; this happens over and over again in history—and the faithful remnant are actually the true chosen people of God; rather than all of Israel, especially those of Israel who stray. The eschatological theme is very familiar to anyone who knows the Abrahamic eschatological frameworks found in Judaism, Christianity, and Islam: the wicked who abandon God are destroyed and the righteous are saved. For example, in the Damascus Document we read:

> At the time of the former Visitation they were saved, whereas the apostates were given up to the sword; and so shall it be for all the members of His Covenant who do not hold steadfastly to these (MS. B: to the curse of the precepts). They shall be visited for destruction by the hand of Belial. That shall be the day when God will visit. (MS. B: As He said,) The princes of Judah have become (MS. B: like those who remove the bound); wrath shall be poured

upon them (Hos. v, 10). For they shall hope for healing but He will crush them. They are all of them rebels, for they have not turned from the way of traitors but have wallowed in the ways of whoredom and wicked wealth. They have taken revenge and borne malice, every man against his brother, and every man has hated his fellow, and every man has sinned against his near kin, and has approached for unchastity, and has acted arrogantly for the sake of riches and gain. And every man has done that which seemed right in his eyes and has chosen the stubbornness of his heart. They have not kept apart from the people (MS. B: and their sin) and have wilfully rebelled by walking in the ways of the wicked of whom God said, Their wine is the venom of serpents, the cruel poison (or head) of asps (Deut. xxxii, 33). (CD, 7–8 [Vermes])

So here we have punishment for the wicked: those who abandon God's covenant. Notice here that the wicked are not necessarily non-Jews, but rather the princes of Judah who rebelled against God. However, for those who keep the covenant, we read:

For all who walk in these (precepts) in perfect holiness, according to all the teaching of God, the Covenant of God shall be an assurance that they shall live for thousands of generations (MS. B: as it is written, Keeping the Covenant and grace with those who love me and keep my commandments, to a thousand generations, Deut. vii, 9). (CD, 7)

. . .

But all those who hold fast to these precepts, going and coming in accordance with the Law, who heed the voice of the Teacher and confess before God, (saying), 'Truly we have sinned, we and our fathers, by walking counter to the precepts of the Covenant, Thy judgements upon us are justice and truth'; who do not lift their hand against His holy precepts or His righteous statutes or His true testimonies; who have learned from the former judgements by which the members of the Community were judged; who have listened to the voice of the Teacher of Righteousness and have not despised the precepts of righteousness when they heard them; they shall rejoice and their hearts shall be strong, and they shall prevail over all the sons of the earth. God will forgive them and they shall see His salvation because they took refuge in His holy Name. (CD, 14)

34

The righteous are those of the Jews who repent of their sins, listen to the "Teacher of Righteousness", and receive forgiveness from God; these ones are the people who will prevail over the sons of the earth and who will see God's salvation. This kind of talk is very familiar to anyone who is acquainted with Jewish apocalyptic literature, or even early Christian literature. But what makes it interesting is that this eschatological talk is found within a document that lays out precepts on how members of its community are to live in their daily lives here and now. The history of the community—as those who hold fast to God's Covenant in the face of apostasy, as well as the future of the community in its eventual salvation and prevailing over the sons of the earth—is intrinsically tied to how the community functions and organizes itself in the present time and place. The formal and informal communism and the religious and ethical practices are explained by the history of the community, and practiced in light of the future salvation of the community; and are contrasted with the wicked greed, selfishness, and violence of those who rebel against God and are due for destruction.

The practices are also tied to the figure of the Teacher, also known as the Teacher of Righteousness. The identity of this Teacher is contested; but what we have is this one individual, who gathers the community and leads them to the right course and establishes a New Covenant. This New Covenant which is not a rejection of the Old Covenant but rather a re-instating of it; according to the Damascus document:

> And as for that which Moses said, You enter to possess these nations not because of your righteousness or the uprightness of your hearts (Deut. ix, 5) but because God loved your fathers and kept the oath (Deut. vii, 8), thus shall it be with the converts of Israel who depart from the way of the people. Because God loved the first (men) who testified in His favour, so will He love those who come after them, for the Covenant of the fathers is theirs. But He hated the builders of the wall and His anger was kindled (MS. B: against them and against all those who followed them); and so shall it be for all who reject the commandments of God and abandon them for the stubbornness of their hearts. This is the word which Jeremiah spoke to Baruch son of Neriah, and which Elisha spoke to his servant Gehazi. None of the men who enter the New Covenant in the land of Damascus, (B I) and who again betray it and depart from the fountain of living waters, shall be reckoned with the Council of the people or inscribed in its Book from the

day of the gathering in (B II) of the Teacher of the Community
until the coming of the Messiah out of Aaron and Israel. (CD, 8)

We see here that the New Covenant that is created by those who join
the community of the Damascus document is seen as a continuation of the
Mosaic Covenant—a covenant that was, according to the Essenes of the
Damascus Document, largely abandoned by most of Israel. The original
covenant was, in a sense, a prototype of the New Covenant. One's faithful-
ness to the New Covenant would determine one's fate when the Messiah
eventually comes. We see here something very similar to early Christianity:
a New Covenant which is continuous with the Mosaic Covenant and an
eventual *eschaton* in which there are those who will be judged and those
who will be saved.

The reason all of this is important is that we need to understand that
the communal economic relationships that were put in place by the Dead
Sea Scroll communities and the Essenes were not separate from their theology; in fact, they were an outgrowth of their theology. It can be easy for
us post-Enlightenment people to think in terms of things being "other
worldly" as opposed to "this worldly"—to think of religion and eschatology
to be "other worldly"; and to think of how communities administer things
to be "this worldly". For the Essenes there was no such dichotomy. What
God did and what Belial (Satan) did was directly tied to social, political,
and economic matters on earth in the here and now. The coming judgment,
which they believed was on its way, did not lead them to passive waiting;
but rather it led to the building of a parallel community: one which mir-
rored the justice and purity of the age to come, as well as the ideal found in
the Law and the Prophets. This is something to keep in mind also when examining the early Christian community—as we will see the early Christians
had a similar connection between theology and the economic practices of
the community.

The relevance of the Essenes to the economic practices of the early
Christians is obvious. They were a Jewish sect which existed around the
same time as the Christians; and they were very similar—both in how their
economic practices were described, and in their eschatological theology.
Thus we have a group to compare with the early Christians that had striking
parallels with them. In fact, it has been suggested—with some positive evidence—that the Essenes may have provided the Christians with their earliest converts. This proposition is not all that surprising given the similarities
between the two groups, both in their social organization as well as their

eschatology. The fact that Qumran was in the vicinity of Jerusalem—where the first Christian community was formed—also lends to the probability that many Essenes would have been exposed to Christianity and found common ground with it.[19]

19. Capper, "The Palestinian Cultural Context of Earliest Christian Community of Goods," 356.

4

Hellenistic Concepts of Friendship, Common Property, and Attitudes toward the Poor

AMONG THE PAGANS, THERE were also found concepts of a community of goods and praise of these concepts. Among many Greek philosophers, there was an idealized form of friendship that, along with mutual love and affection, included the idea of considering all things common property.[1] The idea is captured in the saying "what friends have is common property" (κοινὰ τὰ φίλων). This friendship, however, was conceived of as a horizontal relationship between social equals. Various philosophers, including Plato, Aristotle, Cicero, and Seneca, quote the saying "what friends have is common property" (κοινὰ τὰ φίλων) in one form or another. Aristotle's quote is one of the earliest:

> For in every community there is thought to be some form of justice, and friendship too; at least men address as friends their fellow-voyagers and fellow soldiers, and so too those associated with them in any other kind of community. And the extent of their association is the extent of their friendship, as it is the extent to which justice exists between them. And the proverb 'what friends have is common property' expresses the truth; for friendship depends on community. Now brothers and comrades have all things in common, but the others to whom we have referred have definite things in common—some more things, others fewer; for of

---

1. Ferguson, *Backgrounds of Early Christianity,* 67–68.

friendships, too, some are more and others less truly friendships.
(Aristotle, *The Nicomachean Ethics*, 8.9 [Ross])

Aristotle here recognizes that there are different degrees of friendship; but he presents the ideal community as one based on friendship and common property. This community, however, depends entirely on equal reciprocity, which requires a measure of equality of status. According to Aristotle, when one is superior to another, the superior would rightly expect to receive more from the relationship; whereas what the inferior gets ends up being an act of "public service" by the superior rather than true friendship.[2] Aristotle almost instinctively understands that friendships between people of unequal means almost necessarily turns into a kind of commercial relationship—where each is attempting to exploit the other:

> For they [the superiors] think that, as in a commercial partnership those who put more in get more out, so it should be in friendship. But the man who is in a state of need and inferiority makes the opposite claim; they think it is the part of a good friend to help those who are in need; what, they say, is the use of being the friend of a good man or a powerful man, if one is to get nothing out of it?
> (Aristotle, *The Nicomachean Ethics*, 8.14)

And thus anytime there is an apparent inequality—in wealth, or virtue (often the two are thought to go together in Hellenistic thought)—friendship cannot be expected to exist. Even if there is a friendship which starts out on good and equal grounds; if the balance of wealth or virtue between the parties starts to become one-sided—the friendship ought not to be expected to last.[3]

This concept of friendship or community is not based on an eschatological vision or a messianic hope, which a community (such as that of the Qumran Community) is striving toward or living out. Rather, it is based on simple self-love, the idea being that a virtuous and good man would love himself, and for that same reason, he loves other virtuous and good men. At the same time, lesser men, un-virtuous or wicked men, need not be loved; since they do not have the qualities that would be considered lovable and thus do not meet the requirements of being part of a community of virtuous men. Aristotle's concept of friendship begins with the self: one must start with the building of virtue in one's self and learning how to love one's

2. Aristotle, *The Nicomachean Ethics*, 8.14.
3. Aristotle, *The Nicomachean Ethics*, 8.7.

own virtuous self, and only then can one correctly determine how to find someone who is worthy of friendship:

> Friendly relations with one's neighbours, and the marks by which friendships are defined, seem to have proceeded from a man's relations to himself.
>
> . . .
>
> Therefore, since each of these characteristics [that make one virtuous] belongs to the good man in relation to himself, and he is related to his friend as to himself
>
> . . .
>
> They [the characteristics that make one virtuous] hardly belong even to inferior people; for they are at variance with themselves, and have appetites for some things and rational desires for others. (Aristotle, *The Nicomachean Ethics*, 9.4)

In this view of friendship and common property we have an exchange ethic that is still very much a part of what would otherwise look like communism. The friendship is based on a measurable equality of virtue and wealth (as already mentioned, virtue and wealth were often thought of as belonging together naturally); and the mutual aid and common property envisioned in friendship are really more expressions of self-interest and love of the higher virtues than true communism. It is not so much "from each according to his ability, to each according to his need" as much as it is "from each according to his worth, to each according to his worth."

Cicero, in his thinking of common property, had a very conventional view of the commons and private property—at least in a legal sense. Everything in nature starts out as common property; private property, however, is created through legislation and is necessary for a civilized society to develop. Despite the need for private property, certain things still belong in the commons (water for example); and beyond that, common property is—for the most part—only appropriate among friends. The reason for this is also rather conventional: resources are limited and the poor are many— thus the need for private property law to prevent the poor from eating up all the resources, and a limiting of communist relationships to only those who are friends.[4] His attitude toward what kind of friends can hold things in common is similar to that of Aristotle:

> But of all the bonds of fellowship, there is none more noble, none more powerful than when good men of congenial character are joined in intimate friendship; for really,
>
> . . .
>
> Nothing, moreover, is more conducive to love and intimacy than compatibility of character in good men; for when two people have the same ideals and the same tastes, it is a natural consequence that each loves the other as himself; and the result is, as Pythagoras requires of ideal friendship, that several are united in one. (Cicero, *Duties*, 1.17 [Miller])

For Cicero—just as for Aristotle—friendship, and the common life that follows, is mostly appropriate for virtuous equals. Cicero may be somewhat softer in his tone, but he nonetheless follows the same logic: similarity of ideals and an equivalence of good character lead to being united as one in friendship. Seneca, on the other hand, is somewhat more straight-forward, according to him:

> this community of goods can exist between wise men only, who alone are capable of knowing friendship; the rest are just as little friends as they are partners. (Seneca, *On Benefits*, 7.12 [Basore])

This view can be seen as cynical, but it reflects what educated Greeks would have seen as the reality on the ground. Communism is good, friendship is good, but pragmatically—when it comes to a community of goods— true friendship only works among equals. It cannot reliably cross social or cultural boundaries and certainly not class boundaries. According to these philosophers, human beings are selfish; and the poor and un-virtuous would take advantage of the rich and virtuous if they are given the opportunity. This was the harsh truth as these philosophers saw it. For true friendship to work, the facts on the ground—such as those of wealth, social status, and moral education—had to show that the participants were at least credibly equal. The greater the factual inequality there was, the less likely a credible, principled equality could be established; and this principled equality was

---

4. Cicero, *Duties*, 1.16.

absolutely necessary for a proper friendship to function.[5] For the most part this upper-class communism was informal communism; it would manifest itself as the giving of loans to one another, the giving of gifts to one another, or otherwise sharing informally. There was, however, at least one group who took the concept further: The Pythagoreans.

The ultimate in common life among the educated upper-class Greeks would have been the Pythagoreans, a fact that we recognize when we read Cicero's (as seen above) appeal to them in his discussion of friendship. It was thought that Pythagoras (the founder of the Pythagorean philosophical school) was the one who originally came up with the saying "friends have all things in common"; and that his disciples—being strict ascetics—formed a community that practiced a form of strict, formal communism.[6] In the Pythagoreans, we have a group that seems to have actually put the idealized principle of friendship—with its common property—into tangible practice. Certainly this group would have been praised for putting into real practice what most other philosophers merely wrote about.

That being said, the Pythagoreans were not like the early Christians, nor were they much like the Essenes. The Pythagoreans, like most other Greeks, were not eschatological, nor were they messianic. The members of the ascetic communities of Pythagoreans were privileged and educated philosophers or students of philosophers who were dedicated to learning the (almost gnostic and occult) Pythagorean philosophy. Because of this, membership was more or less limited to the upper classes.[7] Thus the Pythagorean community reinforced the general Hellenistic assumption: communism is good, but it has its place only among the wise and virtuous upper classes. For the philosophers, communism was for the elite. But even the communism of the elite was ultimately based on the logic of self-interest.

The Christians did not limit membership based on social class or philosophical training; Christianity was not a philosophy based around secret knowledge, occult practices or cosmologies—it was a messianic eschatological movement. The Christians, like the Essenes, were messianic, eschatological, and Jewish.

Sharing freely and on equal terms across classes was completely anathema to Greek and Roman culture. Philanthropic giving from the rich to the lower classes—on the other hand—certainly was a pagan virtue, but

5. Verboven, "Friendship among the Romans," 413.

6. Laertius, *Lives of the Eminent Philosophers*, 8.1.10.

7. Huffman, "Pythagoras," 4.3.

it took on a very different form than that of the ideal of friendship. Like many ancient societies, Roman and Greek society was based on norms of reciprocity. A rich man sharing with a poor man, especially when that poor man had no ability to provide the rich man with honor or status, simply made no sense in Greek and Roman culture. However giving, especially large scale civic giving to the lower classes, did make sense if it followed a certain formula. The upper classes giving to the lower classes was always understood to be undertaken in exchange for honor and acclaim from the receiver—this required the receiver's acclaim to be worth something. The formula was this: the rich provide the wealth that they have, giving charity to the lower classes; the less wealthy repay with the honor that they have, bestowing that honor upon the rich. But to give to someone who did not have honor to repay did not make sense; in fact it was considered bad luck to even have a dream where one gave money to a beggar, due to the saying "For Death is like a beggar, who takes and gives nothing in return."[8]

For this kind of giving to work, the rich would have to give to the right kind of lower classes (Roman citizens, freedmen, and so on). For example, the wealthy man would show his civic virtue through lavish displays of giving to the worthy lower classes; those lower classes would reciprocate by bestowing honor upon him—perhaps bestowing on the wealthy man the honor of priesthood, some political office, or a title such as "patron of the city". Here we see the same kind of logic as the logic underlying the concept of "bread and circuses" in the Roman world.[9] This kind of giving re-enforced inequalities and domination rather than uniting people for a common good or uniting people in solidarity. It also split up the lower classes between the worthy lower classes (such as Roman citizens and freedmen) and the unworthy lower classes (beggars, widows, slaves, barbarians, and the truly destitute). Often, this kind of giving manifested itself in the form of a patron-client relationship, a kind of contractual relationship that institutionalized the inequality of status of its participants.[10]

The Greco-Roman patron-client relationship was an informal (personal, not legal or commercial) relationship where the client was basically a kind of servant to the patron and the patron gave gifts or money to the client. Having many clients of worthy station was a sure way for a patron to

8. Brown, *Through the Eye of a Needle*, 76.

9. Brown, *Through the Eye of a Needle*, 63–64.

10. Nicols, "Hospitality among the Romans," 436.

display his high social status.[11] However, this kind of patron-client relationship was not possible for those in extreme poverty, the abjectly destitute;[12] it was reserved for the more privileged of those in the lower classes, or the middle classes, who had the ability to bestow honor on the patron in order to receive material aid—it was a safety net that had a status threshold one had to meet in order to have access to it.[13] Thus very much following the "bread and circuses" kind of logic.

The pagan view of the poor in and of themselves was not flattering. The general view of poverty was that it was something shameful and repulsive, as Greg Woolf writes:

> The poor themselves, abject and repulsive, were made innocuous because less than human and ridiculous. Poetic poverty also offered graphic reassurances of the absolute necessity of material wealth as a precondition of a civilised life. Here it fed on and elaborated the overt role wealth had in structuring Roman society, a role for which the census is a convenient symbol for us as for them. Poverty, finally, was the darkness against which Roman civilisation shone so brightly. For the wealthy, that is.[14]

In other words, the poor were the gross underbelly of what was otherwise a beautiful civilization. There was a material requirement one had to meet in order to warrant human value, those who did not meet that requirement were more an embarrassment than anything else. The kind of poor who were not worthy of philanthropy: the destitute, the non-citizen, the beggar—were not the kind who would benefit from the kind of philanthropy that followed the "bread and circuses" logic or the patron-client kind of relationship. Even philosophers who were more humanitarian in their views of the poor, and who supported philanthropic giving to the poor, limited their support of philanthropy to the "worthy" poor who would fit into the patron-client kind of logic (respectable and virtuous citizens); not the truly destitute.[15] In Plautus's play "Trinummus", the character Philito says:

> He deserves ill of a beggar who gives him what to eat or to drink; for he both loses that which he gives and prolongs for the other a life of misery. (Plautus, *Trinummus*, 2.2 [Riley])

11. Ferguson, *Backgrounds of Early Christianity,* 67.

12. Woolf, "Writing Poverty in Rome," 85.

13. Morley, "The Poor in the city of Rome," 34.

14. Woolf, "Writing Poverty in Rome," 99.

15. Parkin, "'You do him no Service': another exploration of pagan almsgiving," 62.

This encapsulates a common attitude towards the poor and destitute: there is no need to really pay any attention to the truly destitute: they are miserable, wretched, and it is better to simply ignore them. Unlike the more deserving poor, they have no honor to offer, they are beyond any kind of dignity.

For the Greeks and Romans, giving to the poor, and upper-class communism had nothing to do with human equality or solidarity. The upper-class communism reflected the virtues of the upper classes. The philanthropic giving was an exchange of goods for honor, and a cementing of the political and economic power of the rich; it reminded the poor that their well-being depended on the ruling class, and it reminded the ruling class that they had better keep the poor satisfied lest they enrage the mob. Of course, when I say "poor", I mean the poor that mattered: Roman citizens and respectable freemen; the truly destitute do not even enter the picture, they are beyond concern. These expressions of communism and philanthropy had at their root a kind of reciprocity: their moral foundation was primarily that of an exchange relationship. The communism of wealthy social equals came with the expectation of equal levels of sharing (what one gave was expected to be reciprocated equally, if not more so); and the philanthropy of the wealthy to the poor came with the expectation of a bestowal of honor, and a recognition and praise of the wealthy persons superiority.[16]

In examining the Greek "common property" traditions we should remember that the Hellenistic traditions cannot be the main framework from which we examine the early Christian economic practices. The early Christians began among Jews, and they were described as being uneducated— a fact that was used against the early Christians to mock them.[17] Almost everything the earliest Christians did revolved around, and was justified and explained by, the Jewish Bible and the Jewish traditions. By the time Paul came along (which was quite early), the community—with its core practices—was more or less established by its original members.

In addition, the Hellenistic communist traditions were not cross-class: they were meant for the educated and philosophically astute, not for the poor; and poverty did not receive the same focus in the Hellenistic tradition as it did in the Jewish tradition. The early Christians on the other hand, wanted to make sure no one was in need in their implementation

16. Hume, *The Early Christian Community,* 53.

17. Acts 4:13; Origen, *Against Celsus,* 1.9.

of communist relations. Where we do find pagans living out or idealizing perfect virtues of friendship—for example within the Pythagorean communities—they did so for philosophical reasons, not religious reasons, and only among social equals.

That being said, the Hellenistic concepts of common property and friendship, even if they were limited to the upper classes, are relevant when it comes to early Christianity. This is not because they would have had a direct causal effect on Christian economic relationships; but rather because they give us an idea as to how early Christian social life could have been viewed by Greeks. A group of individuals who shared their goods (such as the early Christians) would have been right in line with common concepts of Greek virtuous friendship. Even in the brutal world of the Roman Empire there still was a certain ethic of communism, sharing, and philanthropy which Hellenistic Gentiles were aware of and which many held in high esteem. So when a Greek pagan encountered Christianity and noticed that Christians practiced sharing and common property, there would have been a certain cultural appeal for the pagan, and the practices would have been understood as virtuous.

The strangest thing would not necessarily be that there was sharing, or a community of goods; but rather that it took place across class and across culture—and in a way that put the needs of the truly poor and disadvantaged first (orphans and widows). It comes as no surprise then, that the many among the Greek pagans were attracted to such a unique and revolutionary movement as the Christian movement must have seemed.

The form of "all things in common" that Luke uses, ἄπαντα κοινά, is not paralleled in the Hebrew tradition; it is paralleled, however, in Aristotle's formulation of ἔστι δ' ἀδελφοῖς μὲν καὶ ἑταίροις πάντα κοινά.[18] Also paralleled in Aristotle is the phrase ψυχὴ μία (one soul) which is found in Acts 4:32.[19] Seeing that Luke used forms of these Hellenistic sayings in his descriptions of the economic practices of the early Christians, it would seem that he would have been aware of how these formulations would sound to Greeks, and that they would have the ring of virtue in the ears of those familiar with Greek moral philosophy. It seems that Luke was using sources that appealed to a Hellenistic or an educated audience, or that he himself was appealing to a Hellenistic or educated audience in his descriptions of the economic practices of the early Christians. In fact, all of Luke's writings

18. Aristotle, *The Nicomachean Ethics*, 1159b.
19. Aristotle, *The Nicomachean Ethics*, 1168b.

(the gospel of Luke and the Acts of the Apostles) seem to be written in a way that would be recognized as a Hellenistic historiography, or perhaps a Jewish Hellenistic historiography—especially by a Gentile audience.[20]

This, however, does not justify us reading back Hellenistic traditions into the early Christian economic practices themselves. The Essenes were also described by both Josephus and Philo as having "all things in common"—using the Hellenistic formula. In Luke using versions of the Hellenistic phrase of πάντα κοινά for his descriptions of the early Christians—as well as Philo and Josephus for their descriptions of the Essenes—we understand that Luke, Philo, and Josephus were appealing (at least partially) to a Hellenistic audience. With that knowledge in mind, we can use these Hellenistic traditions of common property to figure out what these writers were attempting to communicate. However, as we already mentioned, the early Christians, like the Essenes, were not educated Greeks; they were mostly uneducated Jews. So we cannot necessarily use the Hellenistic tradition as the primary framework from which we can reconstruct the economic practices of the early Christians; any more than we should use them as the primary framework to reconstruct the economic practices of the Essenes.

20. Witherington, *Acts of the Apostles*, 39.

5

The Economic Practices of the Early Christians

ACTS 2:42–47 AND ACTS 4:32–37

NOW THAT WE HAVE looked at the economic world from which Christianity grew, defined the types of economic relationships by which we can examine communities, and looked at possible parallel groups and concepts in the context of early Christianity—we can take a look at the actual economic practices of the early Christian communities themselves. Our beginning point would naturally be the passages from Acts from which the title of this book is taken:

> They devoted themselves to the apostles' teaching and fellowship, to the breaking of bread and the prayers. Awe came upon everyone, because many wonders and signs were being done by the apostles. All who believed were together and had all things in common; they would sell their possessions and goods and distribute the proceeds to all, as any had need. Day by day, as they spent much time together in the temple, they broke bread at home and ate their food with glad and generous hearts, praising God and having the goodwill of all the people. And day by day the Lord added to their number those who were being saved. (Acts 2:42–47)

. . .

Now the whole group of those who believed were of one heart and soul, and no one claimed private ownership of any possessions, but everything they owned was held in common. With great power the apostles gave their testimony to the resurrection of the Lord Jesus, and great grace was upon them all. There was not a needy person among them, for as many as owned lands or houses sold them and brought the proceeds of what was sold. They laid it at the apostles' feet, and it was distributed to each as any had need. There was a Levite, a native of Cyprus, Joseph, to whom the apostles gave the name Barnabas (which means "son of encouragement"). He sold a field that belonged to him, then brought the money, and laid it at the apostles' feet. (Acts 4:32–37)

Here we have two descriptions of the economic practices of the Jerusalem Christian community.

Both texts include two important details when it comes to the economic practices of the community. The first is the practice of holding all things in common—included in Acts 4 is the statement that no one claimed private ownership of any possessions. The second is the practice of selling possessions and having the proceeds distributed according to whomever was in need. Acts 4 added that the apostles were the ones who did the distributing.

In these two details, we find a similar problem to the one we discussed earlier with the description Josephus gives of the Essenes. How could it be that they held all things in common on the one hand; yet on the other hand, they, as individuals, sold their possessions and had them distributed? In order to answer this let us first examine what was happening in regards to the selling of possessions and the distributing of the proceeds.

Acts 4:36–37 gives the example of Barnabas, who sold his field and handed the money over to the apostles for distribution. Barnabas is a prominent figure in the book of Acts, and this verse could simply be his introduction. Another possible interpretation of this verse is that the selling of fields followed by the handing over to the apostles the proceeds was so rare that when it did happen it was worth mentioning the specific instance. Given the naming of Barnabas, and his importance later on in Acts; as well as the fact that it is only he who is mentioned—I tend to think the former is more likely. That being said, the latter is not impossible given that the number of individuals owning a significant amount of land would presumably have been very small among the early Christians (as it was among the population of first-century Palestine). However, as we see later, this selling and handing over of money involved the transfer of quite a bit of wealth.

When we move on to Acts 5, we come across the story of Ananias and Sapphira. The important part of the story for our purposes is when Peter confronts Ananias over the fact that he had lied about how much of the proceeds—of the field he had sold—were handed over to the apostles:

> "Ananias," Peter asked, "why has Satan filled your heart to lie to the Holy Spirit and to keep back part of the proceeds of the land? While it remained unsold, did it not remain your own? And after it was sold, were not the proceeds at your disposal? How is it that you have contrived this deed in your heart? You did not lie to us but to God!" (Acts 5:3–4)

This clearly shows that the selling of property and the laying of the proceeds at the feet of the apostles was not a systematically enforced program; rather, it was more something which people did of their own accord to support the community. The text also shows us that the proceeds were at the disposal (literally at the authority, ἐξουσίᾳ) of Ananias prior to his handing them over to the apostles. This distinguishes the practice from those of the community described by the Community Rule document and, to a lesser extent, the communities described by the Damascus Document—both of which regulated the use of property among their members.

This account of Ananias and Saphira must not be confused with some kind of *apologia* for private property; as though Luke wanted to make sure his readers did not take what he had previously written in Acts 2:42–47 or Acts 4:32–37 too seriously. The account has a parallel in the book of Joshua with the story of Achan. In that story, God had commanded that everything in the city of Jericho, other than the precious metals (which were to be dedicated to God), was to be destroyed after the city was conquered.[1] After the destruction of the city, Achan took some of what was to be destroyed for himself, hiding it; and because of that disobedience Joshua lost a later battle with A'i. Joshua finds out that he lost the battle because of a sin among the people,[2] and he finds out it was Achan who had sinned. Achan had taken, not only what was to be destroyed, but also what was to be dedicated to God.[3] Therefore, Achan was killed and Joshua was able to prevail against A'i—this time with the permission from God to keep the plunder.[4]

---

1. Joshua 6:17–19.
2. Joshua 7:6–11.
3. Joshua 7:19–22.
4. Joshua 7:26—8:2.

The problem with Achan's actions was his keeping, for himself, something which God had commanded was not to be kept. God had dedicated some things for destruction, and some for himself, and Achan disobeyed, hiding the plunder as though God was not able to see it. If we go back to the account of Ananias and Saphira, we see something similar happening: they held back what was dedicated to the needy among the Christians, hiding what they had held back, as though God did not see it; lying to Peter and the Holy Spirit.[5] After this, Ananias and Saphira were killed; and there subsequently occurred many signs and wonders, and many people joined the community.[6] God was blessing the Christian community just as he blessed Israel under Joshua after Achan was killed.

What was dedicated to the poor in the early Christian community was dedicated to God; lying about what was dedicated to the poor to the apostles was like lying to the Holy Spirit itself. That they had "authority" over the property and proceeds prior to handing it over highlights this very fact, it was up to them to share; just like it was up to Achan to follow God's commandments. Nevertheless, even though it was not the main point of the story, we do see in this account that the selling of property and the giving of the proceeds was not enforced by the Apostles.

This fact gives us another reason to look at the problem of what "all things in common" means. It cannot mean that literally all things in the possession of all the members of the community were literally common property, with the entire community having authority over them; since Ananias was told that he rightly had authority over his land, and even the proceeds of his land before he handed them over to the apostles.

The solution to this apparent contradiction is likely the same solution to the contradiction we spoke of earlier when dealing with the Essenes as described by Josephus. The solution is that there are two aspects being described in Acts 2:42–47 and Acts 4:32–37: informal communism and formal communism. The "all things in common" statement describes a moral disposition that can be described as informal communism. This moral disposition is a view that one's own property is something to be shared, something that is rightly at the disposal of fellow Christians who are in need. Acts 4:32, says that nothing that was possessed by someone was said to be his own (οὐδὲ εἷς . . . αὐτῷ ἔλεγεν ἴδιον). The use of the phrase "said to be his own" gives us a hint that this was not necessarily a systematic rule,

5. Acts 5:2, 8.
6. Acts 5:12–16.

but rather an ethical principle being formed in the community. Had it been a systematic rule it would not be relevant what the property was "said to be", since that would have been decided by the rule. If, on the other hand, it was an ethical principle then what the property was "said to be" would have been the deciding factor dictating the nature of the property.

That Luke uses the Hellenistic formula ἅπαντα κοινά supports this fact. Aristotle and other Greek writers applied the "all things in common" maxim to friendship: a social relationship; not something like the state or a highly regulated institution. So Luke seems to be attempting to convey the idea that the Christians put into practice the Greek ideal of common property among friends—who are of high social status that is—that the philosophers so praised; only they did so cross-class. The early Christian community was as diverse as the world it grew out of; it was not a class based movement.[7] It was this ideal: of perfect friendship—which perhaps was previously only fully in place among the Pythagoreans of old—that the Hellenistic readers of Acts would think of when reading the phrase ἅπαντα κοινά. That this phrase refers primarily to a kind of relationship rather than an institution would by no means diminish its impact on the economic lives of the early Christians.

The Spanish saying "mi casa es su casa" (my house is your house) is a common way of saying that one's guest should make use of one's house as if it were his own. This saying does not mean that the owner of the house is going to change the name on the deed; it is, rather, a declaration of one's willingness to share one's home with one's neighbor, as if it were also their neighbor's house. It is very rare that the saying "mi casa es su casa" is actually taken literally to the point where guests actually treat their host's house as if it were their own. However, what Luke seems to imply by writing "and no one claimed private ownership of any possessions" in Acts 4:32 is that this was taken literally: the Christians really did treat property as though it really was common and no one claimed ownership over their own property. In a sense you could say that, in the case of the early Christians, you might as well have changed the name on the deed. That is how seriously they took their sharing.

In this way, you could have a community that looks exactly like "communism" in the classical Marxist sense of the word—where all property is held collectively—without actually having collective property. It would not be the case that the "communism" starts out by changing the property

7. Fiensy, "The Composition of the Jerusalem Church," 230.

arrangements of the community; and then attempting to adjust the behavior, or way of thinking, of the members of the community. Rather, it would be that the way of thinking and behavior of the members of the community would change first—which would in turn influence the property arrangements of the community as a whole. To understand this process we can take a small scale example: a marriage. When a couple moves in together they may each have their own individual property, the home may be in either the man's name or the woman's name. Over time however, the situation will often change to the point where everything is more or less treated as common property between the two. The situation does not necessarily change because the property arrangements are explicitly adjusted; rather, the couple simply changes their behavior and changes their attitude to the property—which in turn creates a situation that is more or less indistinguishable from the classical Marxist concept of communism.[8]

Looking further into the second century, we get some confirmation of this view of "all things in common" in Justin Martyr's First Apology:

> We who formerly delighted in fornication, but now embrace chastity alone; we who formerly used magical arts, dedicate ourselves to the good and unbegotten God; we who valued above all things the acquisition of wealth and possessions, now bring what we have into a common stock, and communicate to everyone in need . . .
> (Justin Martyr, *First Apology*, 14 [Roberts and Donaldson])

In this passage, holding things in common is associated with a virtue rather than a system. Chastity and Godly dedication are moral principles adopted once a person becomes a Christian, as is holding things in common. The opposite of holding things in common is the acquisition of wealth, or rather, valuing the acquisition of wealth. Had "all things in common" been primarily describing a community institution, rather than an ethical principle; it would not have made sense to include it among things like piety and chastity. Nor would it make sense to speak of "bringing into a common stock" as the opposite of valuing something—such as the acquisition of wealth.

Chastity and piety are virtues that a Christian attains after conversion and spiritual practice and growth. It is the same with holding things in common stock and communicating to those in need. For Justin Martyr, this is a spiritual and moral practice based on Christian virtue.

---

8. Greaber, *Anthropological Theory of Value*, 159–160.

This passage, along with the following passage from Tertullian's apology:

> One in mind and soul, we do not hesitate to share our earthly goods with one another. All things are common among us but our wives . . . (Tertullian, *Apology*, 39 [Thelwall])

tells us that what we are dealing with, in the informal communism of holding all things in common, is much more than simply personal philanthropy. If Tertullian had to distinguish the practice of sharing goods in common with the practices of other groups who shared wives, and concluded that this sharing was a result of being "one in mind and soul"—it becomes clear to us that this sharing went beyond the occasional giving of gifts. One would not generally confuse sporadic personal philanthropy with individuals being so tied together that they are sharing wives; however, the early Christians were sharing to such a degree that Tertullian felt he needed to prevent such a confusion in his apology.

In modern liberal capitalist societies we differentiate between private philanthropy and economics; we also differentiate between completely free actions and mandated actions. As we already discussed in chapter 2 of this book, these differentiations were not so clear in the ancient world. Many modern economic theories are really nothing more than various ways to describe capitalism: whatever falls outside capitalism is not considered economics. But we are not talking here about a capitalist society, so we must be careful to not think in those terms, and to not impose distinctions that did not exist in the ancient world on the ancient world.

The modern notion of freedom, or voluntary action, really comes from a Lockean notion of freedom; where one simply chooses himself, absent any external coercion, what he should or should not do. This concept of freedom puts the whims of the human will as the supreme determining factor of free action. In this model of freedom the will is considered to be sovereign and is obedient to nothing but itself. This concept of freedom allows for the market ideology which views all demands as equal, and quantifiable only through market mechanisms; in the market, the demand for pornography is the same as the demand for medicine—both are desires of the sovereign will. This is not the same kind of freedom that was conceived of in the ancient world; freedom in the ancient context was the ability to pursue virtue—to pursue the Good without obstruction. Much like a sculpture could be spoken of as having been liberated from the marble; human nature was most liberated when it had rid itself of all obstacles that obstructed the pursuit of the Good.[9] Socrates, as portrayed by Plato, provides us with an explanation of a common view of freedom in the Greek philosophical tradition:

> But what about doing wrong? Will the mere not wishing to do it suffice—since, in that case, he will not do it—or does it require that he also provide himself with some power or art, since unless he has got such learning or training he will do wrong? I really must have your answer on this particular point, Callicles—whether you think that Polus and I were correct or not in finding ourselves forced to admit, as we did in the preceding argument, that no one does wrong of his own wish, but that all who do wrong do it against their will. (Plato, *Gorgias*, 509 d–e [Lamb])

This idea of freedom would not include much of what the modern liberal or market ideology would count as freedom. For example, the pornographer creating and selling pornography would not be considered to be exercising freedom in the sense that Socrates understood it. Rather, this pornographer would be going against his will, since no man of sense does something immoral willingly—he would be doing so simply because of a lack of moral training, or the inability to constrain himself. Whereas someone who produced medicine for the benefit of others would be considered to be exercising freedom in that they were aiming toward an end that was inherently good—thus following a will that functioned properly, and was not in error. Socrates is also recorded by Plato as saying:

> For Simonides was not so ill-educated as to say that he praised a person who willingly did no evil, as though there were some who did evil willingly. I am fairly sure of this—that none of the wise men considers that anybody ever willingly errs or willingly does base and evil deeds; they are well aware that all who do base and evil things do them unwillingly; and so Simonides does not say he gives his praise to the person who willingly does no evil, but uses the word "willingly" of himself. (Plato, *Protagoras*, 545 d–e [Lamb])

This points to the idea that a common understanding of freedom included the notion that immoral action was unfree. The modern notion of freedom is often morally neutral, especially when it comes to economics;

9. Hart, *Atheist Delusions*, 21–22.

what matters in economics is self-interest, and self-interest alone. The type of freedom understood in the ancient world, however, was the freedom to pursue a morally good outcome; pursuing an immoral outcome was not freedom, but a mistake.

It is this ancient notion of voluntary action or freedom that we speak of when we say that the informal communism of the early Christian community was voluntary. A Christian freely chooses not to worship idols; but he is not free to worship idols if he desires to, since it would be morally unacceptable to do so. No one forces the Christian to stop worshiping idols, but he must not worship idols. It is somewhat the same idea that is being conveyed when we talk of the informal communism of the early Christians: Christians were obliged, morally, to share things in common, but they were not coerced to do so; which is why Justin Martyr can put together the holding of goods in common with things like chastity and dedication to God. To not practice such things would not be a legitimate exercise of freedom; but rather, a moral error.

This communism was not based on any social contract, nor was it based on mutual interest. This was communism based on the necessity to be righteous before God if one was to be fully a part of the Christian community. It was the religious and spiritual obligation of both the individual and the community as a whole.

In addition to this informal communism, there also was a structure of formal communism (just as with the Essenes). This involved the collection and distribution of funds. As we have already seen in the story of Ananias and Sapphira, the collection was not mandated; it was rather up to the individuals with property themselves to hand over the property or proceeds of the property to the apostles. But looking a little forward to Acts 6, we learn of the extent of the collection and distribution:

> Now during those days, when the disciples were increasing in number, the Hellenists complained against the Hebrews because their widows were being neglected in the daily distribution of food. And the twelve called together the whole community of the disciples and said, "It is not right that we should neglect the word of God in order to wait on tables. Therefore, friends, select from among yourselves seven men of good standing, full of the Spirit and of wisdom, whom we may appoint to this task. (Acts 6:1–3)

There was a daily distribution of food; this tells us that the collections were large enough to facilitate the daily feeding of widows. This was obviously not insignificant, and it was obviously not just a one-time event.

A daily distribution of food to the widows, of which there were both Hebrew and Hellenist, would have required large amounts of funds; funds that would have had to come from Christians with the means to give a significant sum. As we previously established, this was no mere philanthropy; it was not a one-off giving, equivalent to the occasional giving of "bread and circuses" in exchange for honor. Rather, this was a systematic welfare system with its own infrastructure. This is not something that could have been maintained if the obligation to share had been merely voluntary in the modern sense of the word; that is, as something one simply could choose to do or not to do of one's own accord. There was clearly a strong moral obligation to share, a moral obligation on which one's very Christian identity depended, a moral obligation strong enough to facilitate a daily distribution of food to those in need.

That the goods were first handed over to the apostles and later distributed to those in need also points us away from the idea that these actions are to be understood in terms of philanthropy. There was absolutely nothing that would have prevented those who had wealth from handing over material goods directly to those in need; however, the use of middle men avoided economic relationships based on hierarchy or exchange from overtaking the economic relationships of communism. If a wealthy individual gave directly to a poor individual, especially in the first-century context of the Roman Empire; it could easily have been seen as an initiation of a hierarchical patron-client relationship, or the kind of philanthropy where the poor were expected to give special honors to the rich. Or perhaps the poor would, in hopes of receiving more philanthropy, begin to treat the rich as though they were a patron—assigning them a higher honor or giving them a higher position. This situation apparently did come up in some communities outside of Jerusalem, and was addressed in the letter of James—ostensibly James of Jerusalem.[10] Even if it was someone giving to another of a similar social status—if they were not tied to each other culturally or had not internalized the teachings of fellowship of the early Jesus movement—it could easily have been seen as an initiation of an exchange relationship where rapid and equal reciprocity was expected. Or it could have turned into a situation where only those whom the giver thought may be able to reciprocate in

10. James 2:1–13.

the future would receive aid. Having the distribution go through middle men avoided these pitfalls and kept the community moving towards communistic relationships of fellowship and sharing.[11] This arrangement would challenge the dedication of the wealthier members of the community; they were expected to, in a sense, humble themselves before the poor by entering relationships of communism with them and sharing with them—despite the fact that no special honor would be given in return. This directly challenged the patronage and benefaction systems of Hellenistic philanthropy, as well as the Hellenistic concepts of communism for the upper classes, and really demanded a change of attitude and a demonstration of faith from the wealthy among the early Christians.[12]

The passages we have examined in Acts are limited to the first century and Jerusalem. An important thing to remember, however, is that Jerusalem was the starting point of Christianity according to Acts. The Christian community in Jerusalem was considered to be the center of authority for Christian communities worldwide. Thus the letter of James could also claim to be authoritative and binding for all communities as an apostolic decree. (Unlike Paul in his letters—the figure of James did not have to justify his authority in his letter at all, and it was addressed to the entire Diaspora, not just one congregation). Another thing unique to Jerusalem is that it was also the center of the Jewish world, where Diaspora Jews would come to worship—and where they would be exposed to the first Christian community and perhaps join it (this explains why the Hellenists were part of the community in Jerusalem).[13]

THE TEACHINGS AND THE FATHERS

There is plenty of evidence that the economic practices we are discussing spread well beyond Jerusalem and lasted much longer than the first century. As we have already seen in part, we get later attestation of the communistic practices in the second century from both Justin Martyr and Tertullian; but let us look a little further at some passages from these apologists. Justin Martyr gives us a second-century description of the economic practices of the early Christians in his First Apology, where he describes a typical Christian gathering:

11. Malina and Pilch, *Social-Science Commentary on the Book of Acts,* 46–47.

12. Hume, *The Early Christian Community,* 137.

13. Bauckham, "James and the Jerusalem Community," 56.

And we afterwards continually remind each other of these things. And the wealthy among us help the needy; and we always keep together; and for all things wherewith we are supplied, we bless the Maker of all through His Son Jesus Christ, and through the Holy Ghost. And on the day called Sunday, all who live in cities or in the country gather together to one place, and the memoirs of the apostles or the writings of the prophets are read, as long as time permits; then, when the reader has ceased, the president verbally instructs, and exhorts to the imitation of these good things. Then we all rise together and pray, and, as we before said, when our prayer is ended, bread and wine and water are brought, and the president in like manner offers prayers and thanksgivings, according to his ability, and the people assent, saying Amen; and there is a distribution to each, and a participation of that over which thanks have been given, and to those who are absent a portion is sent by the deacons. And they who are well to do, and willing, give what each thinks fit; and what is collected is deposited with the president, who succours the orphans and widows and those who, through sickness or any other cause, are in want, and those who are in bonds and the strangers sojourning among us, and in a word takes care of all who are in need. (Justin Martyr, *First Apology*, 67)

The second sentence in that passage describes informal communism; but later on, what we have defined as formal communism is described. The distribution to the orphans, widows, and those in need—as well as the giving by those who can; were all central parts of the religious ceremony. The whole endeavor was very organized, even to the extent of making sure that those members of the community who were not present got a portion of what was distributed. The collection and distribution also seem to be part of the service; along with readings, prayer, and so on.

Since it is made clear in the passage that what is given is up to the giver, and that what is distributed is systematic and quite widespread (the sick, strangers, orphans, widows, and all in need)—we can surmise that there must have been both enthusiastic encouragement as well as great moral and cultural pressure to give. The picture Justin Martyr paints for us fits completely with what Luke describes in Acts 2 and 4 regarding both the informal communism and the formal communism of the Jerusalem community. In Justin Martyr we see continuity from the first century to the second century, and we see the same kind of economic relationships being developed. Tertullian also gives us a description of the formal communism aspect of the Christian community in his Apology:

There is no buying and selling of any sort in the things of God. Though we have our treasure-chest, it is not made up of purchase-money, as of a religion that has its price. On the monthly day, if he likes, each puts in a small donation; but only if it be his pleasure, and only if he be able: for there is no compulsion; all is voluntary. These gifts are, as it were, piety's deposit fund. For they are not taken thence and spent on feasts, and drinking-bouts, and eating-houses, but to support and bury poor people, to supply the wants of boys and girls destitute of means and parents, and of old persons confined now to the house; such, too, as have suffered shipwreck; and if there happen to be any in the mines, or banished to the islands, or shut up in the prisons, for nothing but their fidelity to the cause of God's Church, they become the nurslings of their confession. But it is mainly the deeds of a love so noble that lead many to put a brand upon us. See, they say, how they love one another, for themselves are animated by mutual hatred; how they are ready even to die for one another, for they themselves will sooner put to death. (Tertullian, *Apology*, 39)

Tertullian makes it a point that the giving, which facilitates the formal communism, was voluntary and not excessive. He does so for good reason. It seems that Tertullian is attempting to differentiate the Christian practice from other cultic or temple practices in which payments were required—some of these cultic practices even generated income for the state.[14] Tertullian made it clear that this was not a "pay for play" religion, thus the insistence on there being no "buying and selling of any sort in the things of God."

But again, we notice the same thing here as we do in Acts 2 and 4 and Justin Martyr's description: what was being given was large enough to actually facilitate a robust, formal welfare system. The welfare system funded burials services; and supported the needs of orphans, the elderly, prisoners, slaves, those who suffered from disaster, and so on. These economic practices, according to Tertullian, were widely recognized by the outside world; he claims that it was commonly acknowledged that Christians love one another, and that this acknowledgement came from non-Christians seeing the concrete practices of sharing, and care for the poor undertaken by the early Christians. For Tertullian and those who observed the early Christians from the outside; the concrete sharing of material goods and care for the poor was inseparable from their love. Love for the early Christians

14. Ferguson, *Backgrounds of Early Christianity*, 182.

was not an abstract feeling, it was realized in the forming of real economic relationships.

These two later sources tell us that these practices lasted through the second century. Also, given that these descriptions were written in *apologias*, written for the sake of non-Christians, we can also assume that Tertullian and Justin Martyr were confident enough to assume that the practices were so thoroughly widespread that a non-Christian could go to any Christian community and see the practices in play. Not only the practices of formal communism in the form of a welfare system involving the giving and distributing of goods; but also the moral framework of informal communism that obligated Christians to share with each other to the point to which it could be said, in all honesty and seriousness—that they held all things in common.

What we can derive from this fact is that this was not a small-scale, short-term, experimental commune; or just a spontaneous out-breaking of sharing and personal philanthropy. This was—and was meant to be—long-term, institutional, widespread, and organized; and it was firmly based on a moral framework of mutual obligations. It was something that a non-Christian could witness with his own eyes and distinguish as a unique feature of the Christian community.

Returning to Acts 2, we see in verse 42 mention of the "teaching of the apostles" (διδαχῇ τῶν ἀποστόλων). One of the earliest non-canonical Christian documents we have is a document by the same title: the "Teaching of the Apostles", or more commonly known as the *Didache* (the Greek word for teaching). It might possibly be the case that the "teaching of the apostles" mentioned in Acts 2 has some connection with some of the teachings that are found in the *Didache* document. But even if there is no connection, the *Didache* is still very relevant as an early Christian document. The *Didache* is basically a list of commandments and practices by which Christians were to live their lives and by which congregations were to conduct their meetings. Part of the document also concerns the economic practices of Christians:

> Give to everyone who asks you, and do not demand it back, for the Father wants something from his own gifts to be given to everyone. Blessed is the one who gives according to the command, for such a person is innocent. Woe to the one who receives it: if, on the one hand, someone who is in need receives, this person is innocent, but the one who does not have need will have to explain why and for what purpose he received and upon being imprisoned will

be interrogated about what he has done, and will not be released from there until he has repaid every last cent. But it has been said concerning this: "Let your gift sweat in your hands until you know to whom to give it." (Didache 1:5–6 [Holmes])

This instruction is given within the larger context of explaining basic Christian ethics. Giving was seen as something basic in Christian morality, along with forgiveness and restraining oneself from lusts. This view of sharing in the *Didache* is paralleled with what we see in the later writings of Justin Martyr—which we examined earlier—in his description of how those who become Christians change from loving the acquisition of wealth to holding all things in common. For the *Didache*, sharing is a moral obligation; and the giving and receiving have serious ethical implications, namely innocence versus penalties. Penalties for those who take more than what they need, and guiltlessness for those who take when they are in need and who give according to the command.

A little bit further on; in a list of precepts in the *Didache* we read:

You shall not hesitate to give, nor shall you grumble when giving, for you will know who is the good paymaster of the reward. You shall not turn away from someone in need, but shall share everything (συγκοινωνήσεις δὲ πάντα) with your brother or sister, and do not claim that anything is your own (οὐκ ἐρεῖς ἴδια εἶναι). For if you are sharers in what is imperishable, how much more so in perishable things! (Didache 4:7–8)

These precepts tied the Christian to his brother, compelling the Christian to share all things with his brother. This passage matches up with Acts 4:32 in that it commands that the Christian should not consider his possessions to be his own; but rather he should consider them to be at the disposal of his brothers and sisters. Thus we see that the informal communism was to be at the level to where property lines became irrelevant. According to Acts, this precept was taken seriously, literally, and was followed by the early Christians. This precept is also paralleled in another, very early, non-canonical Christian document: the *Epistle* of Barnabas:

You shall share everything (κοινωνήσεις ἐν πᾶσιν) with your neighbor, and not claim that anything is your own (οὐκ ἐρεῖς ἴδια εἶναι). For if you are sharers in what is incorruptible, how much more so in corruptible things! (Barnabas 19:8 [Holmes])

Here we have almost the exact same precept: the Christian is to share all things with his neighbor, and not to consider his possession to be his own. Both passages firmly root the justification for this precept in eschatology: the things immortal, or incorruptible. Both the *Didache* and the *Epistle* of Barnabas appear to be coming from the same source (due to the similarity of language); however, that source does not seem to be the book of Acts, or the same source used by Luke in Acts 2:42–47 and Acts 4:32–37. Acts 2 talks about "having all things in common" (εἶχον ἅπαντα κοινὰ) and Acts 4 talks about that which was possessed being "held in common"; the *Didache* and the *Epistle* of Barnabas on the other hand talk about "sharing all things" (συγκοινωνήσεις δὲ πάντα or κοινωνήσεις δὲ πάντα). In saying that no one called their things their own Acts uses a form of λέγω; whereas the *Didache* and the *Epistle* of Barnabas use a form of ἐρέω. Had the *Didache* and the *Epistle* of Barnabas simply been copying from Acts or copying from Luke's source directly—they would have likely used the same language; that they did not tells us that they were likely drawing from similar traditions within early Christianity, not texts. Finally, only the *Didache* and the *Epistle* of Barnabas tie these injunctions to a distinction between the incorruptible and the corruptible (or mortal and immortal); Acts has no such distinction tied in with the practice.

What this means is that the *Didache* and the *Epistle* of Barnabas represent very early (perhaps even first-century) independent (at least independent of Luke's writings and Luke's sources) witnesses to the economic practices of the early Christians. These passages also tell us that the practices of communism were based on injunctions—they were not based on spontaneous acts of love, or merely practical considerations—and they were normative for the Christians. The fact that these precepts had a specific formula—repeated by both the *Didache* and the *Epistle* of Barnabas—tells us that these precepts were common in early Christianity, well known, and widespread.

In a tight-knit community, such as the early Christian community was: a community where people called each other "brother" and "sister"—it would be expected that one would find more examples of informal communism than one would expect in the wider society. In a sense we could say that the early Christian community was formed as a fictive kin group; and generally speaking, communism is the natural relationship among people who consider each other to be kin.[15] When we combine that expectation

15. Hume, *The Early Christian Community*, 112.

with a strong moral incentive to give and to share, coming from Judaism at first and heightened in early Christianity; it is not at all difficult to imagine a situation in which one could say, seriously and honestly—that all things were being held in common, almost literally.

We have to be careful here to not go to the extreme in our thinking. As previously mentioned, the modern notion of "freedom" is not the same as the ancient notion of freedom. These practices were not mere acts of mercy that one chose to participate in, or chose not to; rather, these practices were necessary if one was to remain guiltless. In fact, taking into account Justin Martyr's inclusion of holding all things in common in a list including chastity and avoiding sorcery—we could say that a Christian would have been considered no more free to not practice sharing than he or she would have been considered free to practice fornication or sorcery.

At the same time, we should avoid thinking of these practices as deriving from an enforced system, as in a state system. First of all, the Christian community was not a state, or anything like a state. Second, all the sources make it clear that they were done on the basis of ethical considerations, not institutional rules or laws. So they were not just "my own goodwill" philanthropy; nor were they legally mandated and enforced systems of redistribution. Rather they were practices rooted in a changing of economic relationships on the basis of deep ethical transformations and moral injunctions, which brought about informal communism as well as a form of formal communism in the community.

FELLOWSHIP

If we go back to the text in Acts 2:42 we read that the early Christians were devoted to teaching, fellowship, the breaking of bread, and prayers. In 4:32, we read that they all were of one "heart and soul" and that they had all things in common. The Greek word for "common" is *koina* (κοινὰ), and it is related to the term "fellowship" in Acts 2:42, which is *koinōnia* (κοινωνία) in Greek. Fellowship is a central concept in Christianity; in the first letter of John, we see how closely this concept is associated with being a Christian:

> This is the message we have heard from him and proclaim to you, that God is light and in him there is no darkness at all. If we say that we have fellowship (κοινωνίαν) with him while we are walking in darkness, we lie and do not do what is true; but if we walk in the light as he himself is in the light, we have fellowship (κοινωνίαν)

with one another, and the blood of Jesus his Son cleanses us from all sin. (1 John 1:5–7)

This "fellowship" that a Christian was to have with his brother or sister in Christ was inseparably tied to the fellowship a Christian has with God. This is clear all over the New Testament, especially in the Johannian literature; as well as in Jesus's teachings and Paul's letters. What we also see, however, is that this fellowship was not simply fellow feeling, or spending time with one another: it consisted of a material tying together of goods and possessions.[16]

This would explain why in both descriptions in Acts (as well as for Tertullian), fellowship—or being one in heart (or mind) and soul—is inseparably tied with the sharing of goods. Fellowship, *koinōnia*, necessarily included having goods in common, *koina*.

When Acts 2 and 4 talk about fellowship and being one in heart and soul; included in this, almost by definition, is the sharing of goods: the informal communism of the community. If the early Christians disregarded this informal communism, in a sense, they would be breaking the fellowship which a Christian must have with his fellow Christians. This fellowship can be described as an informal semi-contractual relationship which includes the mutual obligation to share material goods. This can be distinguished from another use of the term "fellowship" which describes the pleasurable fellowship one would have at a social club or gathering, but would not involve the kind of mutual obligation and sharing of resources we find in the kind of fellowship that is used to describe the early Christian economic practices.[17]

In Acts 2:46, we also have the "breaking of bread", this could be taken to refer to the celebrating of the Eucharist (or Lord's Supper). The early Christian "Eucharistic" practices were not only ritualistic or symbolic; but they also included the actual sharing of meals (either with the "Lord's Supper" or in addition to it). We know this because 1 Corinthians 11:17–22 mentions people who abuse the practice by overeating, and Jude 12 and 2 Peter 2:13 speak about people taking part in the meals (described as feasting, συνευωχέομαι) who perhaps should not be doing so (there is no way you can overeat or feast on a small wafer and a sip of wine; thus we can ascertain that actual meals are being discussed). We also get descriptions of

---

16. 1 John 3:17.

17. Malina and Pilch, *Social-Science Commentary on the Book of Acts,* 36.

these communal meals from the Roman magistrate Pliny the Younger[18] as well as various church fathers such as Ignatius,[19] Tertullian,[20] and Clement of Alexandria[21]—they all talk of these meals as actual substantial meals, not just spiritualized rituals.

Therefore, we see that even the Eucharistic practices (at least some of them) in early Christianity involved a physical sharing of goods; the most basic of goods: food. The shared meals were crucial, not only in re-enacting the "last supper"; but also in continuing a Jewish tradition in which the sharing of meals implied a common life and a relationship with God. The tradition of religiously significant shared meals was part of the religious life of almost all Jewish groups.[22] The sacred meals of the Essenes (as mentioned in chapter 3 of this book), for example, were treated as exclusive and especially holy, the same was true of the Pharisees.[23]

Thus the most central Christian ritual, the re-enactment of the last supper, was saturated with the ethic of sharing. Therefore, there can be no separation imagined between the social relationships and economic practices of the first Christian communities; and the religious and spiritual beliefs and practices of early Christianity. The spiritual and religious beliefs and practices motivated and informed the social relationships and economic practices; and the economic practices and social relationships made manifest the spiritual and religious beliefs. As we have just seen, this was even true in the case of the Eucharist—which originally included an actual shared meal enjoyed in common—and was also the most important religious ritual of Christianity.

The tight connection between worship and informal communism explains how the sharing could be so widespread that Luke could say confidently that the Christians held all things in common. It also explains how the giving of goods could be so widespread and plentiful that a consistent welfare system could be put in place.

One of the most striking aspects of early Christianity was its diversity. Christianity was made up of rich and poor, Gentiles and Jews, Romans, Greeks, and barbarians; yet what was important was their unity in Christ, not their social, political, or ethnic background. As we see, even from the

18. Pliny the Younger, *Letters*, 10.96.

19. Ignatius, *Smyrnaeans*, 8.

20. Tertullian, *Apology*, 39.

21. Clement of Alexandria, *The Instructor*, 2.1.

22. Bauckham, "James and the Jerusalem Community," 61.

23. Ferguson, *Backgrounds of Early Christianity*, 515.

book of Acts itself, the cross-cultural aspect of the early Christian economic practices was there from the beginning. The Hellenist Diaspora Jews and the Palestinian Jews who were joined together in the Christian community, all shared together in fellowship—despite cultural and linguistic differences—even before non-Jews were admitted to the community.[24] This makes the systems of informal communism and welfare even more impressive, and in fact may have led to Christianity's rapid growth. The fact that people who were previously complete strangers were treated as though they were kin—and accepted into a community that practiced both informal and formal communism—meant that early Christians were insulated from many of the afflictions the poor in the surrounding culture were under constant threat from; afflictions such as starvation, being sick without access to care, homelessness, and so on.[25] The tearing down of social and ethnic divisions and replacing them with a community based on extreme solidarity and sharing was unheard of in that time; and frankly, is almost unheard of today as well.

Within the Pauline letters we have a concrete example, in 2 Corinthians, of a specific individual who was in need and received support from the Christian communities: none other than Paul himself—though not from the community he was addressing in Corinth:

> Did I commit a sin by humbling myself so that you might be exalted, because I proclaimed God's good news to you free of charge? I robbed other churches by accepting support from them in order to serve you. And when I was with you and was in need, I did not burden anyone, for my needs were supplied by the friends who came from Macedonia. So I refrained and will continue to refrain from burdening you in any way. (2 Cor 11:7–9)

In other Pauline passages[26] as well as the *Didache*,[27] we find out that prophets and traveling preachers had the right to live from the support of the community. As we also saw in Justin Martyr's description of Christian gatherings, "strangers sojourning among us" were included in the distribution. From this evidence, we can see that the system extended beyond the members of the individual communities themselves to include travelers and traveling preachers.

24. Bauckham, "James and the Jerusalem Community," 63.
25. Stark, *The Triumph of Christianity*, 113–114.
26. 1 Corinthians 9:14–15; 2 Thessalonians 3:8–9.
27. Didache 13.

What this means is that the sharing of the early Christians was not motivated merely by mutual fondness, or the fact that people were imminently dependent on one another, or that they knew each other. Rather, it was motivated by deeper moral and spiritual principles; to the point that even individuals (such as Paul) who were just passing through, who could promise nothing material in the way of reciprocal giving or mutual aid— were included in the community of goods.

Within Acts[28] and the letters of Paul[29] we find extensive evidence that traveling preachers (such as Paul) participated in collections from various communities to be distributed to poorer communities. Thus we have formal communism not only in the giving and distribution to the poor within Christian communities, but also between communities. The Romans could speak of the Roman tax being justified by the "Pax Romana"—an order of peace and security that benefited everyone—which the Empire enforced. In a sense it could be said that the universal Christian community did a similar thing, collecting funds from certain communities to give to the poorer communities, and that this practice was justified not through a militarily enforced peace (as was the Pax Romana), but through universal fellowship through Christ.

I do not think it would be unfair to argue that these practices would have almost certainly played a role in the rapid growth and the survival of early Christianity. The sociologist Rodney Stark points out:

> Because theirs were communities of mercy and self-help, Christians did have longer, better lives. This was apparent and must have been extremely appealing.[30]

In times of great economic stress, the early Christians had a place they could turn to, they had a community where the goal was that no one should be in need. This would mean less early death, more thriving families, and healthier people overall. This community would have appeal, not only for the poor who longed for some kind of security and dignity, but also for the rich and middle classes who may have wanted to have a deeper meaning in their lives, and be a part of something larger and virtuous that made a tangible difference in people's lives and society at large—something which the classical pagan cults and the mystery religions did not offer. Empirically, we

---

28. Acts 11:29–30; 12:25.

29. Galatians 2:10; 1 Corinthians 16:1–4; 2 Corinthians 8:1–15.

30. Stark, *The Triumph of Christianity*, 118.

can see that the economic relationships of communism in the early Christian communities worked—Christianity thrived despite persecution, going from a small sect of persecuted Jews to the most important group in the Roman Empire.

In summary, what we can say of the economic practices of the earliest Christians of at least the first two centuries is the following:

1. Within communities there was a morally motivated, extensive, informal communism—which existed to the extent that it could be said in all seriousness that they held all things in common, and that individuals would not say their property belonged only to themselves; but rather also to the other members of the Christian community.

2. Within communities there was a system of formal communism that consisted of individuals selling pieces of property (land or otherwise) and handing over the proceeds to the leaders of the community—who then distributed the proceeds to those in need of material aid.

3. These practices were theologically based and often tied with liturgical practices; including the taking of the Lord's meal, which was accompanied with an actual shared meal (at least in some of the early Christian communities).

4. These practices were widespread within communities across the Roman world, and they were long lasting (at least through the second century) and well organized; they were not sporadic or spontaneous.

5. The sharing (both informal and formal) included individuals within the community of various ethnic backgrounds and class backgrounds and included outsiders who were sojourning with the community.

In the following two chapters I will look at two different lines of evidence that show just how prevalent and how unique the Christian economic practices were. One way we can track how prevalent the systems of sharing were is by looking at what regulatory frameworks were constructed to protect them, and as we shall see, there certainly were regulatory frameworks in place.

6

"The Tragedy of the Commons"
Dealing with Freeloaders

WHEN YOU HAVE AN extensive welfare system, such as the ones found among the early Christian communities, there is always going to be the possibility of abuse. This is especially the case when the system applies across all kinds of cultural, ethnic, class, and even linguistic lines; such as was the case among the early Christians. Within the New Testament itself, there are clear signs that there was a perceived threat of abuse and that measures were taken in order to prevent abuse from occurring. This is most clearly seen when we are dealing with documents written by Christians for other Christians, that is, documents that were written not to impress or proselytize non-Christians; but rather to deal with issues internally within the community. We would not expect to find Christians shouting from the rooftops to non-Christians about the internal problems of their communities, but we would expect them to be internally addressing those issues among themselves.

An example of a perceived threat of abuse of the economic practices of the Early Christian community being addressed is found in 2 Thessalonians:

> Now we command you, beloved, in the name of our Lord Jesus Christ, to keep away from believers who are living in idleness and not according to the tradition that they received from us. For you yourselves know how you ought to imitate us; we were not idle when we were with you, and we did not eat anyone's bread without paying for it; but with toil and labor we worked night and day, so that we might not burden any of you. This was not because we do not have that right, but in order to give you an example to imitate.

70

> For even when we were with you, we gave you this command: Anyone unwilling to work should not eat. For we hear that some of you are living in idleness, mere busybodies, not doing any work. Now such persons we command and exhort in the Lord Jesus Christ to do their work quietly and to earn their own living. Brothers and sisters, do not be weary in doing what is right.
>
> Take note of those who do not obey what we say in this letter; have nothing to do with them, so that they may be ashamed. Do not regard them as enemies, but warn them as believers. (2 Thess 3:6–15)

None of this admonition would have been necessary had it not been possible for some within the community to eat without working. From this passage we can deduce the extent of the informal communism and the strength of the formal communism. The sharing was so substantial that, in Thessalonica at least, there were individuals who were taking advantage of the common fund, the distribution, and perhaps even the moral obligation of informal communism—without themselves contributing to the community or internalizing their own obligations.

Interestingly, Paul claims that he had a right (or authority, ἐξουσίαν) to receive aid from the community (as we mentioned in the previous chapter of this book). This right seems to be a right reserved for traveling preachers. This is confirmed in a passage found in the *Didache*:

> But every genuine prophet who wishes to settle among you is worthy of his food. Likewise, every genuine teacher is, like the worker, worthy of his food. Take, therefore, all the first fruits of the produce of the wine press and threshing floor, and of cattle and sheep, and give these first fruits to the prophets, for they are your high priests. But if you have no prophet, give them to the poor. If you make bread, take the first fruit and give in accordance with the commandment. Similarly, when you open a jar of wine or oil, take the first fruit and give it to the prophets. As for the money and clothes and any other possessions, take the first fruit that seems right to you and give in accordance with the commandment. (Didache 13)

The teachers had a right to the "first fruit". This is a concept going all the way back to the Mosaic Law.[1] Nevertheless, there was a potential threat that people who travelled around to different communities would take advantage of their hospitality. We notice here that the welfare system not only

---

1. Deuteronomy 18:1–8; 26:1–15.

included outsiders and travelers, but did so to the extent that there was the threat—if not the reality—of people faking being "prophets" so as to take advantage of the system. (We will read about one example of this very activity in the following chapter of this book). We know that today people scam insurance schemes, people scam welfare systems—but it is extremely difficult to scam random acts of giving; the fact that people were scamming Christian communities implies that these communities had implemented something similar to an organized welfare system. Just as Paul lays out instructions to prevent abuse, so does the *Didache*:

> If the one who comes is merely passing through, assist him as much as you can. But he must not stay with you for more than two, or, if necessary, three days. However, if he wishes to settle among you and is a craftsman, let him work for his living. But if he is not a craftsman, decide according to your own judgment how he shall live among you as a Christian, yet without being idle. But if he does not wish to cooperate in this way, then he is trading on Christ. Beware of such people. (Didache 12:2–5)

This sheds some more light on what Paul said in 2 Thessalonians. Paul was an artisan, he worked for his living; however, he also had a right to receive support from the community should he choose to accept it. Others who were travelling and sojourning among the Christian communities who did not work as artisans or craftsmen would have to do something to help in the community before they would have a right to material aid. However, they would then certainly have a right to that material aid; they would have a right to share in the community of goods—including the expectation of support as well as access to the general sharing, or the informal communism—of whatever Christian community they were visiting..

The fact that we find such strict regulations on what happened with the distribution shows that the distribution was significant enough that it could be taken advantage of. The fact that there were work requirements also shows us that the access to the material aid was significant enough to warrant such a requirement.

The formal communism was so significant that Luke—in Acts 4:34—could rightly say that there was not anyone needy among them. This statement could easily be taken as an idealized exaggeration; but, given the clear indication that restrictions on abuse needed to be made and enforced, it should be read as an actual historical description. In fact, as already pointed out, this expansive, organized distribution could be one of the reasons that the movement grew as fast as it did in the early years. The Christians may have been seen as a reformation movement, putting into practice the biblical ideal of shared prosperity for all.[2] This evidence points us away from the notion that the statement "there was no one needy among them" was just an idealized exaggeration, and points toward the idea that Luke is describing an actual historical situation of communist economic relationships that could have been witnessed by Christian and non-Christian alike. No idealized exaggeration requires checks and balances; but extensive systems of formal communism do.

Further evidence for the large scope of the formal communism comes from the first letter addressed to Timothy. In 1 Timothy 5:4–8 the children and grandchildren of widows are admonished to care for their mothers or grandmothers; in rather strong language. The widows, however, are admonished to be pious and to not live for pleasure. The purpose of this admonition is made clear in verse 9:

> Let a widow be put on the list[3] if she is not less than sixty years old and has been married only once; (1 Tim 5:9)

Directly after this passage more requirements are given for the widows to be put on the "list"; and if you read from verse 10–14, you can see that the requirements are quite stringent. Some of those requirements were that the widows on the list were to have been long-term members of the community and that they themselves were known to have aided others in need in the past. This "list" brings us back to Acts 6:1–6; where men are appointed to care for the daily distribution to the widows, a distribution that had apparently sometimes favored the Hebrews over the Hellenists, and thus required that the apostles assign people to make sure this did not happen. This letter tells us that the distribution to widows was not only happening in Jerusalem, nor did it only happen right after Pentecost; rather, it was widespread and long lasting.

We also learn—from the fact that strict requirements for the widows were put in place, and strong admonition was given to the family members of the widows to care for their widowed relatives—that this distribution was significant enough to cause some people to consider handing over the care of their widows to the Christian communities they were part of. Given

---

2. Evans, *From Jesus to the Church*, 105.

3. "be put on the list"—καταλεγέσθω—according to Thayer's Greek Lexicon can refer to military enrollment; this implies organization and structure.

that to be included on the "list" the widows had to have been long-term members of the community and have been known to help others in need in the past—we can assume that some widows may have even gone so far as to pretend to be Christians, or to convert for less than pious reasons, in order to be part of the distribution.

From the examples that we have in the *Didache* and Paul's letters we see that many problems stemming from the tragedy of the commons would come primarily from outsiders coming into the community. I am using the term "tragedy of the commons" in the sense that Garrett Hardin, the originator of the term, used it:

> The tragedy of the commons develops in this way. Picture a pasture open to all. It is to be expected that each herdsman will try to keep as many cattle as possible on the commons. Such an arrangement may work reasonably satisfactorily for centuries because tribal wars, poaching, and disease keep the numbers of both man and beast well below the carrying capacity of the land. Finally, however, comes the day of reckoning, that is, the day when the long-desired goal of social stability becomes a reality. At this point, the inherent logic of the commons remorselessly generates tragedy.[4]

As we can see Hardin assumes that the herdsmen treat each other as strangers and potential enemies. Had they been treating each other as neighbors, they would have likely cared about their neighbor's access to the commons and cared about how they were perceived by their neighbors— and thus regulated their use of the commons. In other words, they would have had a measure of trust for one another.

Informal communism almost always happens between individuals— or within communities—that are close, have some kind of common interest or common life experience, and who trust one another. Whereas exchange relationships are generally reserved for strangers who are not able to trust each other and who suspect that the other is willing to take advantage of any generosity shown.[5] When a communist relationship is applied to people who consider each other as strangers, as potential enemies, and when resources are limited; there is a real possibility of the "tragedy of the commons" becoming a reality. For example, I might be more willing to lend my bike to a neighbor, or to buy a beer for someone who speaks my language when I am in a foreign land; than I would be to lend my bike to a stranger,

4. Hardin, "The Tragedy of the Commons," 1244.
5. Graeber, *Debt*, 33–35; 116.

or buy a beer for someone who speaks a completely different language. Christianity however—quite early on, or at least starting with Paul, was a universalist religion—by which I mean specifically that the community was tied together, not by common interests in land, language, or nationality; but rather only by the fact that they recognized Jesus as their lord. (Of course, members might originally have been drawn to the Christian community by such ties of affiliation with others, such as the household of Cornelius).[6]

This creates a problem. The Christian was expected to share with both the neighbor who lives in the same area, belongs to the same community, speaks the same language, and is of the same social class and ethnicity as himself; and also the Christian who may be of a different ethnicity and a different social class, who speaks a different language, and comes from a faraway land. The problem is that outside of one's dedication to being subject to Christ, there would be no social pressures that would naturally prevent someone who does not share various other aspects of common life—such as ethnicity, language, class, and so on—from taking advantage of Christian sharing. (The reason I will not lend my bike to a stranger as opposed to my neighbor, is that there is less social pressure on him not to steal my bike than there is pressure on my neighbor). Thus there was the pressing need for rules and regulations to prevent abuse, and this is what we find in Paul's letters and the *Didache*.

Of course, this problem is generally offset in cultures that strongly encourage hospitality. Hospitality (literally love of strangers, φιλοξενία) was encouraged in early Christianity, as it was in Greco-Roman society.[7] However, Christianity included individuals coming from different cultures; and these individuals were tightly tied together despite their cultural differences. Thus, in order to have real communistic practices and still have a universal, cross-cultural, and cross-class community—there would need to be rules; the fact that there were such rules points to the fact that there were substantial communistic practices among the early Christians. Even though encouraging hospitality would have offset some cultural differences and threats of abuse, the rules and regulations needed to be in place to take care of what the ideal of hospitality alone did not.

Another way to track the prevalence and uniqueness of the Christian economic practices is to examine how the early Christian communities looked to the non-Christian world.

6. Acts 10.

7. Nicols, "Hospitality among the Romans," 436.

7

The View from the Outside

WHEN YOU WANT TO know what a certain family is like, you would do well to not only ask the members of the family, but also to ask people outside the family. A family can say "we are a really loving family" and that might be how they feel; but getting the outsider's view will allow you to balance the family's view of themselves with that of the outsider in order to get a more accurate picture of what the family is like. It may be the case that they fight all the time and the neighbors hear them. Even so, the family may prefer to be thought of as a loving family; so it would be smart to ask the neighbors as well as the family to get the whole picture (of course taking the limits and biases of the neighbors into account as well).

When it comes to the economic practices within the early Christian communities, there are a few outside sources that we can turn to in order to examine how they looked to non-Christians. The first source I want to look at is the second-century writing called the "Passing of Peregrinus", written by the Greek satirist Lucian. In this writing, a cynic philosopher called Peregrinus Proteus travels around and stays with different Christian communities, soon realizing that he can take advantage of them.

In this writing, the Christians are portrayed as so naïve and gullible that Proteus manages to trick them into thinking that he is some kind of prophet or legitimate leader. He managed to do this by basically spending time with the Christian leaders, reading their books, and interpreting and preaching on them.[1] Proteus is then taken by the authorities and imprisoned because of what he was doing with the Christians; which almost ap-

---

1. Lucian, *The Passing of Peregrinus*, 11.

pears as a benefit to his scam in that he could portray his imprisonment as a righteous act of martyrdom to the Christians he was scamming. In fact, Lucian describes the fact that Proteus was arrested as "an asset for his future career". The Christians then spend their time providing for him in prison; giving him food, money (described as "not a little revenue" by Lucian—the narrative portrays it is a significant amount), comfort, and visitation. The Christians are described as caring for him all day, reading for him—and even using the common funds to pay for Christians from other cities to come and encourage Proteus.[2]

Lucian then goes on to mockingly explain what Christian doctrine is:

> Furthermore, their first lawgiver persuaded them that they are all brothers of one another after they have transgressed once, for all by denying the Greek gods and by worshiping that crucified soph- ist himself and living under his laws. Therefore they despise all things indiscriminately and consider them common property, re- ceiving such doctrines traditionally without any definite evidence. So if any charlatan and trickster, able to profit by occasions, comes among them, he quickly acquires sudden wealth by imposing upon simple folk. (Lucian, *The Passing of Peregrinus*, 13 [Hamron])

After Proteus is released, Lucian says about him:

> He left home, then, for the second time, to roam about, possesing an ample source of funds in the Christians, through whose min- istrations he lived in unalloyed prosperity. (Lucian, *The Passing of Peregrinus*, 14)

What is interesting about Lucian's description is that he takes the Christian practice of sharing—the informal communism of the com- munity—and treats it as something stupid, equating it with "despising all things." This practice was, according to Lucian, one of the main traits of the Christians, and it was a sign that they were not to be taken seriously and could easily be exploited.[3]

This tells us a few things. One is that the practices of sharing were something that clearly made the Christians stand out in comparison with the larger society. It was not that they were simply being hospitable in the normal way good and polite people of that time would recognize as

2. Lucian, *The Passing of Peregrinus*, 12–13.

3. Interestingly enough in the *Wars of the Jews* (2.8.2 §122) Josephus describes the Essenes as despisers of wealth, thus giving us another parallel between the Essenes and early Christians.

appropriate hospitality, and idealizing it in their writings. Their practices also were not general philanthropy from the rich to some of the poor, as would have been recognized as normal for wealthy and virtuous men. This was a full-scale shift in the economic relations among the Christians that could be clearly seen from the outside and was identifiable as a uniquely Christian practice.

It also tells us that the precautions given by both Paul and the *Didache* against freeloaders were certainly needed—given how easy it seemed to be for a huckster like Proteus to take advantage of the Christians. The amount of money Proteus could gain from the scam was significant; it was large enough for Proteus to make a career out of taking advantage of the Christians' common funds and practices of sharing. Another thing we learn is that the enemies of Christianity recognized the sharing that the Christians practiced, and these enemies thought of it as something negative. They did not try to deny it, they did not try to diminish it; rather, they mocked it as something stupid. Had these practices been something that Christians only wrote about, rather than practice, Lucian would have probably found something else to mock them for, or called them out as hypocrites for preaching a way of living they did not actually practice.

Lucian's description shows us just how strange the economic practices of the early Christians looked to outsiders. The Christians seemed to be despising all things through sharing. Lucian simply could not fathom why anyone of sense would throw caution to the wind and actually hold all things in common, especially when it included sharing with strangers and the truly needy—unless they despised property and/or were simply stupid. Lucian's view of what the Christians were doing fits with the general view educated Greeks had of communism and the poor as we discussed in chapter 4 of this book. It also shows us that, for Lucian, this is what made people Christian: this was one of the major features of the Christian community that differentiated it from the wider society.

This was a bold move for Lucian since what the Christians were doing could have been seen as virtuous to some outsiders. As we read in chapter 4 of this book many educated Greeks held certain types of communism in high esteem. Highlighting the communism of the Christians would not have been Lucian's first choice as something to mock; unless, that is, this communism was an unmistakable reality among the Christians that no one could deny; and was really done to a degree that it was seen as strange and over the top.

Another opponent of Christianity who wrote on this matter was the fourth-century pagan Roman emperor known as Julian the Apostate. Of the sources we are looking at, Julian is the latest and the most prominent in status. At this point in history, Christianity had grown significantly. There already had been two Christian emperors and Christianity was now a major religious movement, but Julian was intent on reviving the old pagan gods.

Both the Roman world and Christianity were very different in the fourth century than they were in the first and second-centuries; but nonetheless, I include Julian as an outside source because of the uniqueness of having a pagan emperor writing about the Christian economic practices— as well as his frankness and honesty. We cannot necessarily translate what Julian writes back to what Luke was describing in Acts; but we can see how a pagan emperor viewed the economic practices of at least some of the Christian communities in the fourth century. Among our sources for Julian the Apostate's views of Christianity are some of the letters that he wrote. One such letter was written to someone named Hecebolius:

> Therefore, since by their most admirable law they [the Galilaeans] are bidden to sell all they have and give to the poor that so they may attain more easily to the kingdom of the skies, in order to aid those persons in that effort, I have ordered that all their funds, namely, that belong to the church of the people of Edessa, are to be taken over that they may be given to the soldiers, and that its property be confiscated to my private purse. This is in order that poverty may teach them to behave properly and that they may not be deprived of that heavenly kingdom for which they still hope. (Julian the Apostate, *Letters*, 40 [Wright])

The Galilaeans (the name Julian uses for Christians) were selling things and giving to the poor to such an extent as to elicit a response from the emperor himself. The response was that the state should confiscate the funds of the church (likely the common funds that are kept on behalf of the poor, so here we are talking about the formal communism aspect of the community) and expend them on the Roman military.

From this letter we get further insight into how the theology of the Christians was seen from the outside. Julian seemed to think that Christians would sell their goods and give to the poor in order to get into the kingdom of heaven. This is easy to understand, given gospel accounts such as Jesus meeting the rich young ruler[4] or Jesus meeting Zacchaeus;[5] and it seems that there were at least some Christians who interpreted these passages in such a way that it would be easy to understand why Julian thought that the rich would need to sell their goods and give to the poor to get into the kingdom of heaven.[6] But he also thought that Christians believed poverty to be a virtue, which led him to the sarcastic little joke at the end of the letter—basically saying that once he takes the money from the Christians (thus making then poor), they will be able to get into the kingdom of heaven on account of their poverty.

We understand here that, to the outside world, the Christians were characterized as loving poverty. Again, as seen in chapter 4 of this book, sharing across classes was simply not considered rational, and giving to the poor without reciprocated honor made no sense. Julian's only explanation for Christian sharing is that the Christians simply wanted to be poor, why else would they do something so obviously against their material interests. Their sharing of goods and concern for the poor were also understood by Julian to be intrinsically tied to their religious beliefs and spiritual practices.

Like Lucian, Julian simply cannot understand why these Christians would be doing such things as sharing with the poor. Both Lucian and Julian basically attribute these practices to some kind of superstition, some kind of stupidity or insanity (hating all things equally and loving poverty are both pretty close to insanity). From these sources we understand just how uncanny the practices were to those outside the Christian community; and just how visible and profound they were to the outside as well.

Another Letter Julian wrote addressing the matter was to the high priest of Galatia, Arsacius:

> For it is disgraceful that, when no Jew ever has to beg, and the impious Galilaeans support not only their own poor but ours as well, all men see that our people lack aid from us. (Julian the Apostate, *Letters*, 22)

Here we see the emperor's frustration. Julian complains that the Christians were supporting—not only the poor among them—but also the non-Christian poor. (He also mentions that Jews also take care of their own). This is embarrassing for Julian since among the pagans there was no

---

4. Luke 18:18–29; Matthew 19:16–22; Mark 10:17–22.

5. Luke 19:1–10.

6. For example see Irenaeus, *Heresies*, 4.12.5.

culture for sharing and redistribution to the poor (outside of the patron-client kind of hierarchical relationships, or the "bread and circuses" kind of giving); a fact that put him at a disadvantage in his efforts to re-establish the old Roman pagan cults in comparison with Christianity and its ethic of sharing. In fact, Julian later instructs the priest to try to push into the pagan theology some principles of mutual aid so as to try to get pagans to start helping each other, and especially the poor; even if such a theology was not clearly warranted within the pagan system:

> Teach those of the Hellenic faith to contribute to public service of this sort [the sort practiced by Christians], and the Hellenic villages to offer their first fruits to the gods; and accustom those who love the Hellenic religion to these good works by teaching them that this was our practice of old.

> . . .

> Then let us not, by allowing others [specifically, Christians] to outdo us in good works, disgrace by such remissness, or rather, utterly abandon, the reverence due to the gods. If I hear that you are carrying out these orders I shall be filled with joy. (Julian the Apostate, *Letters*, 22)

This was a private letter from the emperor to a high priest. There was no need for Julian to be diplomatic, and the emperor could say exactly what he felt. It seems as though the economic practices of the early Christians were so visible, so extreme, and so different from the greater society that they were making the pagans look bad by comparison. Julian's letters confirm for us that the economic practices of the early Christians were successful: they led to thriving communities with widespread appeal.

The view from the outside is extremely important in order to get a fully rounded picture of the early Christian communities. Christian writers may be motivated to play up their traditions of mutual aid and sharing, but pagan writers had no such motivation. Therefore we see that what was happening was not only significant; it was significantly different from the norm—it was widely seen and recognized, it was theologically based, it was long lasting, and it was an identifying mark of the Christians.

From Lucian in the second century to Julian in the fourth, the Christian practices of informal and formal communism confused and frustrated their pagan neighbors. They thought of the Christians as an anomaly, a strange sect that practiced something previously unknown to the world, a sect that practiced something that made them seem like they had lost their senses, but yet thrived. Looking back, we can see that the economic practices of the Christians were a defining mark and an integral part of their Christian identity and community. We also see that these economic practices were a radical form of sharing that deeply changed the social and economic relationships of the Christians, and everyone could see it; even those that thought they were ridiculous.

8

The Theological Origins of Christian Sharing

JESUS AND THE THEOLOGY OF
THE JUBILEE AND SABBATICAL

THESE INTERESTING AND NEW communist economic relationships and practices did not just come out of nowhere. They came directly from the teaching of Jesus (and were expressed in the theology of Paul as well), which itself was firmly based in the Jewish tradition and in the Hebrew Bible. The book of Acts (in which we find the first direct references to these practices) was written by the same author as the Gospel of Luke. In this Gospel we find recorded many principles from the teachings of Jesus that likely formed the basis for the later economic practices of the Jerusalem community.

In Luke, Jesus begins his ministry in a synagogue in Nazareth:

> When he came to Nazareth, where he had been brought up, he went to the synagogue on the sabbath day, as was his custom. He stood up to read, and the scroll of the prophet Isaiah was given to him. He unrolled the scroll and found the place where it was written:
>
> > "The Spirit of the Lord is upon me,
> > because he has anointed me
> > to bring good news to the poor.
> > He has sent me to proclaim release to the captives
> > and recovery of sight to the blind,

> to let the oppressed go free,
>
> to proclaim the year of the Lord's favor."

> And he rolled up the scroll, gave it back to the attendant, and sat
> down. The eyes of all in the synagogue were fixed on him. Then he
> began to say to them, "Today this scripture has been fulfilled in
> your hearing." (Luke 4:16–21)

This scripture is a quotation of Isaiah 61 and 58. The quotation of Isaiah 61 includes a reference to the "year of the Lords favor", in other words, the Jubilee. Jesus's quotation of Isaiah 58 also references the Sabbatical year law in that it promises a release for the captives and freedom for the oppressed. The Jubilee year (found in Leviticus 25) was held every fifty years (after seven Sabbatical years) and it consisted of the wholesale redistribution of all (non-urban) property back to the family inheritance, leaving the land fallow, and freeing Israelite slaves The Sabbatical year (mentioned in Leviticus 25, but mainly in Deuteronomy 15) was held every seven years and it consisted of a debt release and the freeing of all Hebrew slaves. Both laws put a lot of emphasis on the importance of the obligation that each Israelite has towards his neighbor.[1]

Declaring the Jubilee, and referencing the Sabbatical—at a time when the poor were being constantly dispossessed; at a time when the Roman authorities, wealthy landowners, and aristocrats were enriching themselves at the cost of the poor—could have been seen as a very dangerous and revolutionary declaration. This declaration, in many people's ears, would have amounted to an announcement of a new regime; a regime that would undo the entire economic system that existed in first-century Palestine—a system that enriched the aristocracy at everyone else's expense—and replace it with the ideals of the Jubilee and Sabbatical laws. The captives were to be freed, the debts would be canceled and the land would be redistributed.[2]

Nevertheless, it was not merely a political-economic declaration; the Jubilee and Sabbatical laws were not just mechanisms for promoting economic justice and preventing poverty—they were also ways that Israel would show that they recognize that it is God himself to whom the land belongs and in whom they trust.[3] So ultimately, these laws were not only about love of neighbor; but also about love of God. The logic goes

1. Leviticus 25; Deuteronomy 15:1–18.

2. Yoder, *The politics of Jesus*, 32.

3. Leviticus 25:23–24; Deuteronomy 15:5–6.

something like this: the God of Israel cares about justice and cares for the poor, and those who live on his earth are foreign residents borrowing the land from him; therefore the God of Israel has the right to demand that the land and resources be distributed in a fair way as defined by God himself.

The theology and politics of the Sabbatical year law made their way into the book of Jeremiah, where the prophet Jeremiah blames Judah's coming exile into Babylon on Judah having ignored the Sabbatical year law by not granting the release of slaves and debts. In a condemnatory oracle in Jeremiah 34; God, through the prophet, recognizes that the people declared "liberty"—but then condemns them for having taken back their slaves after having released them in the Sabbatical.[4] At the core of this oracle was the idea that the declaration of the "liberty" should actually have the intended economic consequences on the ground. It was not enough to simply declare "liberty" and continue business as usual. The actual release of debts and of slaves was necessary.

In 1 Kings 21, we find a story involving the Jubilee in the context of a commoner, Naboth, resisting the powerful but corrupt king Ahab and losing his life because of it. Later his death is avenged through a man of God. The story goes like this: Naboth had a vineyard close to the palace of King Ahab; Ahab wanted to buy it, but Naboth refused, citing the law of the Jubilee that states that the land should not be sold on a permanent basis (see Lev 25:23). The idea here was not simply that Naboth wanted to keep his vineyard and Ahab wanted to take it; but rather that Naboth wanted to be faithful to the Jubilee law, a law with the intention of preventing the unequal accumulation of wealth.[5]

Seeing her husband depressed because of Naboth's refusal to break the Jubilee law and sell his land; Ahab's Phoenician wife Jezebel has Naboth killed and Ahab finally gets the vineyard he wanted. But the story does not end there. Elijah finds out about this murder and dispossession and curses both Ahab and Jezebel. Later on, Ahab is killed in a battle with the King of Aram—and much later Jezebel is killed by God's anointed king of Israel: Jehu; thus finally avenging Naboth.[6]

This account puts the Jubilee in a new light; showing how the Jubilee could have been seen as a safeguard for the poor against abuse from the powerful, and that its being ignored could lead to God's judgment on the

---

4. Jeremiah 34:13–17.

5. 1 Kings 21:1–4.

6. 2 Kings 9.

powerful who ignore it. The story of Naboth is one where the poor could hope in the protection of the Jubilee legislation; and when that legislation was violated, hope that justice could be restored—for example by God's anointed, such as someone like Jehu. This story certainly would have appealed to the Galilean and Judean peasantry in the first century who were undergoing constant dispossession and oppression at the hands of the ruling classes and likely longed for a release in the form of something like a Jubilee.

As discussed in chapter 1 of this book, when the rebellion in Jerusalem broke out in the sixties C.E., one of the first actions of the rebels was to burn down the debt records; a few decades before that, Judas the Galilean had led his rebellion against the Roman census. It could be argued that both rebellions had something to do with the theology of the Jubilee and Sabbatical laws. The census, which Judas the Galilean rebelled against, would have brought Roman property law into Israel; making land distribution something which was not God's business (as it would have been if the Jubilee law was followed), but the Roman state's. The burning of the debt records by the rebels in the sixties C.E. could be seen as a cancelling of the debts as mandated by the Sabbatical law.

The dream of re-establishing the Jubilee and enforcing the Sabbatical—of bringing about a community of justice and righteousness, free from Gentile domination—was clearly alive and kicking around the time of Jesus and of the birth of Christianity.

The language of the Sabbatical year law is directly paralleled in Luke's description of the Christian community's economic practices in Acts 4. Acts 4:34 begins:

There was not a needy person among them

Which in the Greek reads:

οὐδὲ γὰρ ἐνδεής τις ἦν ἐν αὐτοῖς

In the description of the Sabbatical year, Deuteronomy 15:4 begins:

There will be no one in need among you

Which, in the Greek Septuagint translation (which was the Bible of the early Christians), reads:

ὅτι οὐκ ἔσται ἐν σοὶ ἐνδεής

The Septuagint says there will be (ἔσται being the future tense of εἰμί) no one in need (ἐνδεής); whereas Luke declares that there was (ἦν being the aorist past tense of εἰμί) no one in need (ἐνδεής)—a term which only appears in this instance within the New Testament; yet appears three times in the Greek Septuagint rendition of Deuteronomy 15.[7] This connects, linguistically, the description of the economic practices of the early Christian community directly with the Sabbatical law. I do not think it is a mistake that the declaration by Jesus which references both the Jubilee and Sabbatical laws is recorded by the same writer who first records the economic practices of the Christians in Jerusalem, and who records these practices in a way that brings to mind the Sabbatical law as recorded in the Septuagint. In his popular commentary on Acts, N.T. Wright writes:

> Jesus had, after all, announced as his agenda (in Luke 4) the programme of 'Jubilee' set out in Isaiah 61, and had gone around talking about forgiveness both of sins and of debts. Now his followers were, in the most practical way possible, making real the implied promise of covenant renewal. Not only would they forgive debts every seven years; they would not keep their own private property to themselves, but would share it in common.[8]

So what we are seeing, in Acts 2 and 4, is simply a practical working out of Jesus's program, a renewal of the covenant and a putting into place the principles of the Sabbatical and the Jubilee laws in a practical and concrete way. What Deuteronomy said will be the case with God's people, actually was the case with God's people after Jesus had made his declaration referencing the Jubilee and Sabbatical laws and the early Christians had put the principles of the Jubilee and Sabbatical laws into practice through their communist economic relations.

When Jesus made his declaration in Luke 4, he was understood as saying that the time had come to realize the goals of the Jubilee and Sabbatical laws and the social ethics held within them: to make the goals of the Jubilee and Sabbatical laws into a reality.

This kind of declaration, appealing to the Jubilee and Sabbatical laws, would not necessarily have been a completely novel idea. It was part of the messianic expectation for many Jews in Palestine at the time. Evidence of this can be found in at least two documents from the Dead Sea Scrolls: the Melchizedek Document (11Q13) and the Messianic Apocalypse (4Q521).

---

7. Hume, *The Early Christian Community,* 138.

8. Wright, *Acts for Everyone Part 1,* 75.

The Melchizedek Document describes Melchizedek as a messianic figure, and this messianic figure is the one who will bring about the Jubilee:

> And concerning that which He said, In this year of Jubilee each of you shall return to his property (Lev. xxv, 13); and likewise, And this is the manner of release: every creditor shall release that which he has lent [to his neighbour. He shall not exact it of his neighbour and his brother], for God's release has been proclaimed (Deut. xv, 2). And it will be proclaimed at the end of days concerning the captives as He said, To proclaim liberty to the captives (Isa. lxi, 1). Its interpretation is that He will assign them to the Sons of Heaven and to the inheritance of Melchizedek; for He will cast their lot amid the portions of Melchizedek, who will return them there and will proclaim to them liberty, forgiving them the wrong-doings of all their iniquities. And this thing will occur in the first week of the Jubilee that follows the nine Jubilees. And the Day of Atonement is the end of the tenth Jubilee, when all the Sons of Light and the men of the lot of Melchizedek will be atoned for. And a statute concerns them to provide them with their rewards. For this is the moment of the Year of Grace for Melchizedek.
>
> . . .
>
> those who uphold the Covenant, who turn from walking in the way of the people. And your ELOHIM is Melchizedek, who will save them from the hand of Belial. (11Q13, 2 [Vermes])

For the writer of the Melchizedek document, the Jubilee was more than a piece of economic legislation from the Torah; it was also an eschatological sign for what the future savior (represented as Melchizedek) would accomplish. The Jubilee was not only economic, but also spiritual; its enactment forgave inequities and saved the pious from Belial.

The Messianic Apocalypse gives us a similar description of what the coming of the Messiah would accomplish:

> the heavens and the earth will listen to His Messiah, and none therein will stray from the commandments of the holy ones. Seekers of the Lord, strengthen yourselves in His service! All you hopeful in (your) heart, will you not find the Lord in this? For the Lord will consider the pious (*hasidim*) and call the righteous by name. Over the poor His spirit will hover and will renew the faithful with His power. And He will glorify the pious on the throne of the eternal Kingdom. He who liberates the captives, restores sight to the blind,

straightens the bent (Ps. cxlvi, 7–8). And for ever I will cleave to the hopeful and in His mercy . . . And the fruit . . . will not be delayed for anyone. And the Lord will accomplish glorious things which have never been as He . . . For He will heal the wounded, and revive the dead and bring good news to the poor (Isa. lxi, 1). . . . He will lead the uprooted and make the hungry rich . . . (4Q521, 2 [Vermes])

Neither the Jubilee or the Sabbatical are directly referenced here, but Isaiah 61 is—the same scripture that Jesus quotes in his mission statement recorded in Luke 4, and the same scripture the Melchizedek Document quotes in reference to the Jubilee. In this document, we see that the Messiah's coming has everything to do with the renewing of the poor, bringing good news to the poor, and making the hungry rich. The kingdom of God, brought by the Messiah in this document, is a kingdom that brings about economic restoration and brings to reality the principles underlying the Jubilee.

These two documents shed light, not only on Jesus's declaration referencing the Jubilee and Sabbatical laws, but also his disciples' response to it and their messianic hope—they show us the ideological context through which Jesus's declarations would have been interpreted. Jesus's declaration, his messianic claims, and his declaring God's kingdom were all linked together; many of his disciples would have heard him loud and clear as saying that this was the time when things were going to be different for the poor, and the economic realities were about to change. These changes were certainly going to be terrestrial, in the here and now; but also cosmic and eschatological in the future.

This was not only a matter of Jesus making a single declaration in the synagogue of Nazareth and then his followers, after Jesus's death and resurrection, coincidentally putting that declaration into practice in the form we find recorded in Acts 2:42–47 and Acts 4:32–37. Rather, it appears there was a "Jubilee and Sabbatical theology" which permeated Jesus's entire ministry, inspiring his followers and impressing on them the "Jubilee and Sabbatical mindset".

JESUS TEACHES THE JUBILEE
AND SABBATICAL IN PRACTICE

One clear example of this "Jubilee and Sabbatical mindset" is found in Jesus's Sermon on the Plain in Luke 6:20–49. First we have, in verse 20–26, the Blessings and Woes—where "woe" is declared for the rich, the full, and those who laugh; but fullness, happiness, and blessing is declared for the poor, the hungry, and those who weep—because society is about to be flipped and the social order is going to be reversed (which is what happens in the Jubilee with the redistribution of the land; as well as with the Sabbatical in the releasing of debts and slaves). Starting in verse 27, Jesus explains what the moral consequences of the Jubilee/Sabbatical reversal are to be. The moral consequences of the Jubilee and Sabbatical reversal involved an ethic of sharing; in verse 30 he commands that one should "give to everyone who begs from you," and then further he says:

> If you do good to those who do good to you, what credit is that to you? For even sinners do the same. If you lend to those from whom you hope to receive, what credit is that to you? Even sinners lend to sinners, to receive as much again. But love your enemies, do good, and lend, expecting nothing in return. Your reward will be great, and you will be children of the Most High; for he is kind to the ungrateful and the wicked. (Luke 6:33–35)

In verse 30, the term "give" ($\delta i\delta\omega\mu\iota$) is used in reference to what we might today call "charity": simply giving to someone who begs, or someone in need. In verse 33–35, however, the term "lend" ($\delta\alpha\nu\epsilon i\zeta\omega$) is used. This is not what we would call charity; this is a relationship usually found among individuals who consider one another, at least theoretically, as equals; a relationship where one would expect a return of what was borrowed.

However, Jesus's admonition is to lend without expectation of return. A gift does not necessarily tie individuals together; but it can, in some cases, create a sense of superiority and inferiority. A gift could be seen as a way to show one's superiority over an inferior by suggesting that the gift was a demonstration of a benefaction, which the giver may have held back; in a sense, it could be seen as an attempt to demonstrate that the receiver of the gift depends on the giver for his well-being.[9] It could also be seen as a way to make someone "owe" something to the giver on the giver's own terms; thus a debt would be made in which the giver could decide what a satisfactory repayment would be (an example of this in popular culture might be the portrayal of a mafia favor; where a mafia gangster does a favor for someone; but in accepting that favor there is an implication that sometime in the future the gangster may call on that someone to do a favor in return—usually a favor that heavily outweighs the original favor from the mafia gangster in

9. Graeber, *Debt*, 116.

its consequence).[10] When a gift is given by an inferior to a superior, the gift could be seen as constituting an obligation—something that is now regularly owed to the receiver ("you gave me that last time, so why not now?"). In many ancient and mediaeval societies, a gift given to a king, or a lord, could end up being treated as a precedent, as a custom, that resulted in that gift becoming an obligatory tribute demanded by the king or lord.[11]

The risk of a gift turning a relationship that might have been primarily based on relationships of informal communism into relationships based on hierarchy would be especially heightened when one party has more wealth than the other. The less wealthy person receiving the gift may want to avoid being seen as inferior by quickly repaying the gift; either with something equivalent or something of higher value; thus turning the relationship into one of exchange rather than hierarchy or communism. Thus a communist relationship could easily turn into exchange when it is based on gift giving between people who are of unequal means; since there may be the fear that the gift giving could turn the relationship into a hierarchical one with the one of lesser means being the inferior party.[12] This was a very real possibility in the early Christian community, given that it was made up of both wealthy and poor individuals.

Lending, however, implies an on-going relationship between people who relate to each other as social equals and who trust one another. This of course is only true when what is lent is not calculated or measured, and the "debt" is not enforced; but rather based on mutual trust. Debt where what is lent and what is owed is measured is markedly different from the kind of uncalculated "debt" that ties people together in relationships based on communism. Calculated debt is really just a time extended market exchange; whereas the kind of "debt" that results from lending to someone without expecting a return is not really a "debt" in the way we think about it at all, rather it is just a general moral obligation to treat the giver in kind. That kind of "debt" or moral obligation resulting from something being lent without it being calculated generally implies a communist relationship is being formed, since it demonstrates that the lender is willing to trust the receiver.[13] David Graeber puts it this way:

10. Graeber, *Debt*, 108.

11. Graeber, *Debt*, 110.

12. Greaber, *Anthropological Theory of Value*, 221; 225.

13. Graeber, *Debt*, 79.

> The difference between a debt and an obligation is that a debt can be precisely quantified.[14]

To illustrate the difference between the social consequences of an uncalculated loan as opposed to a gift, consider the difference between someone buying you a beer, you saying "thanks", and the other person saying simply, "you're welcome", without any engagement; compared to the other person replying, "don't worry, you can get me back some other time" and allowing for the formation of a relationship. The latter reply puts you on the road to a relationship that we might characterize as informal communism—the person buying you a beer has shown that he wants to you and him to be friends, the kinds of friends that buy each other drinks; and as a friend you have an obligation to treat him as that kind of friend. Unless, that is, you immediately reciprocate by buying the person a beer and thus avoid any future obligation; or, unless you make it clear that you will repay the person with something of absolute equal value (for example by asking for the price of the beer and promising to repay the exact price in cash) and thus making the relationship one based on exchange—where a calculated reciprocity replaces the implied trust of communism.

The former reply, on the other hand, may be taken as just an altruistic gift, without any obligation to maintain the relationship or reciprocate in any way. Alternatively, the former reply could cause some suspicion that the person who bought you a beer is trying to make it a point that he is buying people drinks; trying to show off, or demonstrate that he has so much money that he can throw it around and spend it recklessly. Or, in some cultures, receiving a gift that does not involve any obligation to mutual aid, could be seen as a sign that you are accepting a position of lesser dignity than the giver.[15]

The sort of relationships involving mutual obligation built up through lending without taking accounts and sharing will almost always put people in relationships of informal communism—relationships that function on the basis of an assumption of permanence (as mentioned in chapter 2 of this book). To Quote David Greaber again:

14. Graeber, *Debt*, 21.
15. Graeber, *Debt*, 105.

The surest way to know that one is in the presence of communistic relations is that not only are no accounts taken, but it would be considered offensive, or simply bizarre, to even consider doing so.[16]

As soon as the debt starts to be calculated, the relationship moves over to exchange; and it then sheds any need for trust and mutual obligations. But this outcome was avoided when Jesus commanded that his followers should lend without expectation of return. The lending in this case does not turn into the grounds for an exchange or a hierarchal relationship. This was to be lending done without taking an account, lending freely—it was based on mutual obligation and trust; rather than lending which included the taking of accounts. Because it was lending, as opposed to a gift—which could imply or result in a hierarchical relationship—it implied, and would result in, a communist relationship based on trust and mutual obligations.

My claim here is not necessarily that Luke had in mind the anthropological categories of social relationships when recording the words of Jesus; rather it is simply that Jesus's teachings—saturated with the ethics and theology of the Jubilee and Sabbatical laws—naturally resulted in the promotion of a certain kind of relationship and avoided others. The Sabbatical year law in Deuteronomy 15 was about the releasing of debts, not about the giving of gifts—thus it avoided certain implications that "gifts" might have had in a culture in which the patron-client relationship was common. If that law was to be followed, then lending without expecting a return would make complete sense—since the debts were going to be released anyway there would be no point in calculating what was loaned in order to receive it back. Jesus's declaration in the synagogue of Nazareth, along with Jesus's command to lend without expecting a return, echoing the Sabbatical year law, would almost necessarily end up in communism if followed.

In Luke, Jesus specifically contrasts the kind of community he wanted to establish with a hierarchical kind of "philanthropic" relationship:

> But he said to them, "The kings of the Gentiles lord it over them; and those in authority over them are called benefactors [εὐεργέται can also be translated "philanthropists"]. But not so with you; rather the greatest among you must become like the youngest, and the leader like one who serves. For who is greater, the one who is at the table or the one who serves? Is it not the one at the table? But I am among you as one who serves. (Luke 22:25–27)

16. Graeber, *Debt*, 99.

The fact that Jesus contrasts the service that his followers are to give to one another with the "philanthropy" of the Gentile kings, shows that Jesus specifically wanted to distinguish the relationships of informal communism that his teachings would produce with the hierarchical philanthropy of the ruling classes. The term εὐεργέτης (used in the plural form εὐεργέται by Jesus and translated as benefactors) was often used to honor powerful individuals who had done something good for their community;[17] in other words, it represented the "bread and circuses" kind of philanthropy, or the patron-client logic discussed in chapter 4 of this book. The patron-client or "bread and circuses" kind of philanthropy was exactly not what Jesus was promoting: Jesus was promoting a Jubilee and Sabbatical ethic, not the hierarchical ethics of the Gentiles that demanded honor in exchange for material aid.

If we look back to Luke 6:33–35 we can see Jesus insisting that his followers nurture relationships of informal communism. Through his admonition to love one's enemies, it seems that he expected his followers to nurture the same kind of relationships even with those whom they normally would not have an informal communist relationship with; as though they were lending to those people with the coming of the Jubilee and the implementation of the Sabbatical in mind, when debts would be canceled anyway and the land redistributed.

When we look at other key passages in Luke, such as Luke's rendition of the Lord's Prayer, keeping in mind the Jubilee and Sabbatical laws; they look a whole lot more "this worldly" then they otherwise might. For example Luke renders the Lord's Prayer:

> He said to them, "When you pray, say:
>
> Father, hallowed be your name.
> Your kingdom come.
> Give us each day our daily bread.
> And forgive us our sins,
>   for we ourselves forgive everyone indebted to us.
> And do not bring us to the time of trial." (Luke 11:2–4)

In the prayer, our sins (ἁμαρτίας ἡμῶν) being forgiven is directly related to our forgiving all who are in debt to us (παντὶ ὀφείλοντι ἡμῖν); in other words, our obeying the Sabbatical law. If we also take into account

17. Lowe, "Paul, Patronage and Benefaction: A "Symbiotic" Reconsideration," 6.

that the land is to lie fallow during the Jubilee year (as well as in the Leviticus version of the Sabbatical year)—which means the farmers would need to rely on and trust God for their food—then the whole Prayer can be seen as a Jubilee and Sabbatical prayer.[18]

This pattern repeats itself all over the Gospel of Luke, such as in the parable of the two debtors who are forgiven,[19] or the parable of the unrighteous steward,[20] and many other passages in Luke.

Often when reading these passages we may face the temptation either to spiritualize them, or individualize them; to turn "debt" into "offense" or "sin", or to assume that all that is being talked about economically is the occasional individual act of philanthropy. However, given the socio-economic context of the time, with debt and dispossession being such a huge problem, along with the Jubilee and Sabbatical traditions within Judaism—there is no reason to believe that these sayings would not have been taken as literal and revolutionary by their original audience: calling for an entirely new way that individuals ought to relate to one another economically. The Lord's Prayer, just to take one example, distinguishes clearly between sin and debt, but relates them to each other: the spiritual and the socio-economic are intrinsically intertwined.

JOHN THE BAPTIST, JAMES, JOHN, AND JOSEPHUS

Even before Jesus's declaration in the synagogue of Nazareth and his teachings on sharing, we have the ground being laid by John the Baptist. His teachings are recorded in the Gospels and Josephus. Luke gives us probably the best summary of his teachings:

> John said to the crowds that came out to be baptized by him, "You brood of vipers! Who warned you to flee from the wrath to come? Bear fruits worthy of repentance. Do not begin to say to yourselves, 'We have Abraham as our ancestor'; for I tell you, God is able from these stones to raise up children to Abraham. Even now the ax is lying at the root of the trees; every tree therefore that does not bear good fruit is cut down and thrown into the fire."

18. Yoder, *The Politics of Jesus*, 62.

19. Luke 7:41–43, notice that forgiveness of debt ties people together in love.

20. Luke 16:1–13, a very strange parable, but if we understanding it in light of the Sabbatical year law, it makes sense—the steward releases debts so as to reconcile himself to the debtors, so that they will also share with him when he needs help; knowing that the total release is at hand and he must rely on his fellow Israelites rather than his position.

And the crowds asked him, "What then should we do?" In reply he said to them, "Whoever has two coats must share with anyone who has none; and whoever has food must do likewise." Even tax collectors came to be baptized, and they asked him, "Teacher, what should we do?" He said to them, "Collect no more than the amount prescribed for you." Soldiers also asked him, "And we, what should we do?" He said to them, "Do not extort money from anyone by threats or false accusation, and be satisfied with your wages." (Luke 3:7–14)

Here we have presented a common theme found in many Jewish prophets, from Elijah up to the prophets of Jesus's day. We find an eschatological declaration along with a call to repentance and a call to bring one's life and social relations into congruence with the way God desires the righteous to live and to relate to others. Part of that call includes honesty on the part of tax collectors and soldiers; but also an implementation of the ethic of informal communism found in verse 11. There, John the Baptist commands a form of "from each according to their ability to each according to their need," using coats and food as the example. If one has two coats and/or has food, and sees someone else that does not—it is one's obligation to share with him.

Just as for the Essenes and Jesus, for John the Baptist this obligation was put in a place of utmost importance because God's kingdom and his concomitant judgment were on their way; the world was going to be put right, and those who desire to be on the side of righteousness cannot rely on the fact that they are Jews for their salvation: they must live in community and deal with each other in line with God's righteousness. For John the Baptist, as for the Essenes and Jesus, this includes repentance; in other words, changing how one lives and relates to one's neighbor.

After John, Jesus came into the picture. Jesus in the gospels is described as not only making the same declarations and giving the same prescriptions as John, but going even further, claiming that he himself is the Messiah who will bring about the kingdom of God. John says that the time is coming—but Jesus says both that it is coming and that it is here.

Very much related to the ethics of the Sabbatical year law and the ethics of sharing, is the question of violence. Just as hierarchy and exchange relationships are predicated on the possibility of violence or actual violence (as we saw in chapter 2 of this book); calculated debt (which is a form of exchange) and violence also often appear together: they are related phenomena—if not out and out violence, then at least the potentiality of violence.

When the debt shifts from being uncalculated and general to being calculated and specific; it shifts the relationship from being one based on communism, where mutual aid is expected; to just an uncompleted exchange relationship, where a determined reciprocity is delayed, but nonetheless expected and enforced by the threat of violence.[21]

If one member of a society inflicts violence on another, or destroys another's property; that one can no longer be trusted to be part of a communist relationship, and the victims will likely want revenge, and a cycle of violence may ensue. In order to avoid such a cycle of violence, the larger society may impose an exact penalty equivalent to the damage done, in order to appease the desire for revenge—thus creating a calculated debt. Having the debt calculated allows both parties to reduce the relationship to pure mathematics, so as to avoid dealing with each other as friends or neighbors, and if the payment does not match up to the debt, it being calculated and recorded gives the justification for the violence that ensues. Not respecting one's obligation in a communist relationship amounts to just being a bad neighbor; not respecting one's obligation in an exchange relationship is a breach of contract that justifies retaliation.[22] As we saw in chapter 1 of this book, the violence of the Roman state and its ability to demand the payment of taxes, along with the ability of landowners to call on the state if rents were not being paid—were necessary factors in the rise of debt and dispossession among the poor.

The connection of calculated debt and even the creation of markets with violence was something well known in the ancient Jewish world. Evidence of this can be found in Josephus's telling of the story of Cain and Abel. Most of his rendition of the story is similar to the story in Genesis: both brothers offer a sacrifice to God, God is only pleased with Abel's sacrifice, Cain gets jealous and kills Abel, and then Cain is banished by God and must wander the land.[23] But Josephus offers some additional details:

> And when Cain had traveled over many countries, he, with his wife, built a city, named Nod, which is a place so called, and there he settled his abode; where also he had children. However, he did not accept of his punishment in order to amendment, but to increase his wickedness; for he only aimed to procure everything that was for his own bodily pleasure, though it obliged him to be

21. Graeber, *Debt*, 14; 77; 121.

22. Graeber, *Debt*, 61–62.

23. Genesis 4:1–16.

injurious to his neighbors. He augmented his household substance with much wealth, by rapine and violence; he excited his acquaintance to procure pleasures and spoils by robbery, and became a great leader of men into wicked courses. He also introduced a change in that way of simplicity wherein men lived before; and was the author of measures and weights. And whereas they lived innocently and generously while they knew nothing of such arts, he changed the world into cunning craftiness. He first of all set boundaries about lands: he built a city, and fortified it with walls, and he compelled his family to come together to it; and called that city Enoch, after the name of his eldest son Enoch. (Josephus, *Antiquities*, 1.2.2 [Whiston])

In Josephus's telling of the story, the man who invented violence (Cain) also seems to have invented the profit motive and markets; violence, markets, and the profit motive are all related phenomena in this tradition. This makes complete sense if we realize that calculated debt and exchange happens (within a community) only when an individual does not trust his fellow and assumes that his fellow will try to take advantage of him; whereas informal communism happens when individuals are in a relationship of trust and mutual obligation with each other and at peace as "neighbors".[24] The sorts of relationships involving markets and profiteering begin when one of the parties shows a willingness to use violence. When the possibility of violence is in the picture, informal communism—with free sharing and uncalculated lending—cannot happen; so instead markets and contracts must take its place so as to avoid out-and-out violence.

With that in mind we can understand why, in the Sermon found in Luke 6, an admonition against violent retaliation[25] is linked to exhortations to lend freely without demanding a return. Violence and retaliation must be banished in order to make room for a situation where informal communism can flourish. There are plenty of other verses found in the Gospels that record Jesus preaching non-violence, and this gives evidence that the admonitions against violence and for sharing were part of the same message.[26]

In Genesis, the story of Cain and Abel directly follows that of Adam and Eve. It could be said that the story of Cain and Abel displayed the result of the introduction of sin into the world by Adam and Eve; which was, according to the tradition recorded by Josephus, physical violence and

24. Graeber, *Debt*, 34.
25. Luke 6:28–29.
26. Matthew 26:52; 5:9, 38–41; John 18:36.

economic exploitation. When the Messiah came to establish the kingdom of God, part of that effort would be to undo the results of sin—including violence and exploitation.

If we lay out and examine all this evidence, we can understand how the economic practices of the early Christians came entirely from the early understanding of the teachings of Jesus and the theology of the kingdom of God. John the Baptist came with his preaching, some of which involved an ethic of sharing based on the eschatological hope of the kingdom.[27] Then Jesus comes and announces the the fulfillment of scriptures involving the Jubilee and Sabbatical laws,[28] he then goes on to teach an ethic based on the Sabbatical and Jubilee laws: an ethic of sharing, a social reversal, self-sacrifice, and non-violence.[29] Jesus identifies himself as the Messiah: the one who will bring about God's kingdom,[30] and he declares that he is the son of man who will stand at the right hand of God as king. Jesus is then killed, buried, and resurrected.[31]

After the death and resurrection of Jesus, the disciples understood that the death and resurrection of Jesus changed everything; and that because of the resurrection, Jesus truly is the king of God's kingdom and the promised Messiah.[32] They also understood that the time for universal restoration, a reversal of the effects of sin, and the coming of the Kingdom was in the near future and that Jesus was waiting in heaven for that time; but until that time comes, the people of God are to repent of their sins and live for the kingdom of God while living out its values in community.[33]

Given this framework, it would make complete sense that the disciples would—in expectation of the *eschaton*—start to implement the principles of the Jubilee and Sabbatical laws in the here and now, while waiting for the universal restoration in the future. The word repent (μετανοέω in Greek) means to change one's mind, literally "with consideration".[34] The idea is that with Jesus's death and resurrection, the coming of the kingdom of God has been verified and the "year of the Lord's favor" is now at hand; so everyone

27. Luke 3:2–14.

28. Luke 4:16–21.

29. Luke 6:20–49.

30. Luke 9:18–20.

31. Luke 22:63—24:12.

32. Acts 2:14–36.

33. Acts 3:17–26.

34. According to Strong's Concordance.

had better act accordingly and change how they relate to God, to the world, and to each other. What we find in Acts 2:42–47 and Acts 4:32–37 is therefore not surprising at all; it is simply the result of Jesus's declarations and his teachings.

Further theological clues can be found in the term "fellowship" used in Acts 2:

> They devoted themselves to the apostles' teaching and fellowship, to the breaking of bread and the prayers. (Acts 2:42)

In 1 John, we get a little theology of "fellowship":

> This is the message we have heard from him and proclaim to you, that God is light and in him there is no darkness at all. If we say that we have fellowship with him while we are walking in darkness, we lie and do not do what is true; but if we walk in the light as he himself is in the light, we have fellowship with one another, and the blood of Jesus his Son cleanses us from all sin. (1 John 1:5–7)

We looked at this passage, along with the term "fellowship" (κοινωνία), in chapter 5 of this book; but now we are going to look at it from a slightly different angle. Fellowship with God is tied with walking in the light and having fellowship with one another. John then continues to explain what walking in the light entails, and in the third chapter, he spells out the fellowship believers are to have with one another in practical terms—linking it directly with the death of Jesus:

> We know love by this, that he laid down his life for us—and we ought to lay down our lives for one another. How does God's love abide in anyone who has the world's goods and sees a brother or sister in need and yet refuses help? (1 John 3:16–17)

The fellowship that John is talking about includes sharing with those in need, and it is closely tied to the sacrificial death of Christ. For John, the death of Christ and its atoning value, impels Christians to be in fellowship with one another and demands that this fellowship be a concrete material one—involving mutual aid.

Jesus declares the that the scriptures in Isaiah 58 and 61 are fulfilled, preaches an ethic of sharing, and announces the kingdom of God with himself as messianic king. Then, in the ultimate act of love, he gives his own life for his people, sacrifices himself for the atonement of others; in order that everyone else may participate in his righteousness. This is, in a sense,

Jesus showing what the kingdom of God looks like: self-sacrifice on behalf of others; it is the king leading the way in showing how his followers are to relate to one another.

Given that the economic practices originated in Jerusalem, and the community in Jerusalem was led by James, we should also look at the letter with the name of James attached to it to see if it can give us further clues to these practices. The Letter of James has many parallels to the teachings of Jesus, which should not be surprising; especially if the letter in fact came from Jesus's brother, who would have known Jesus's way of thinking in an intimate way.[35] The letter of James is very vocal on economic matters. For example, there is James's scorn of the rich, something which James had in common with his brother Jesus, along with a sense of solidarity with the poor.[36] This is certainly in line with the idea that communities that are to be righteous ought to care for the poor and have no one needy among them; along with the idea, common in prophetic Jewish scripture, that the poor are oppressed by the rich.[37]

One of the most important passages relevant to our discussion in the letter of James is found in the first chapter of James:

> Religion [θρησκεία, which can also be rendered worship] that is pure and undefiled before God, the Father, is this: to care for [ἐπισκέπτεσθα, literally "to visit"] orphans and widows in their distress, and to keep oneself unstained by the world. (Jas 1:27)

The important part here is that to visit orphans and widows in their distress, and to care for them, is part of pure worship. (In the Hebrew Bible the phrase "orphans and widows" is often used as a catch-all term for the disadvantaged in society). What keeping oneself "unstained by the world" refers to is clarified immediately afterwards:

> My brothers and sisters, do you with your acts of favoritism really believe in our glorious Lord Jesus Christ? For if a person with gold rings and in fine clothes comes into your assembly, and if a poor

---

35. For example compare: James 5:1–6 with Luke 6:24; James 4:17 with Luke 12:47; James 5:2–3 with Matthew 6:16; James 5:9 and 4:12 with Matthew 7:1; James 3:19 with Matthew 5:9; James 3:12 with Matthew 7:16; James 2:13 with Matthew 5:7; James 2:19 with Matthew 5:19; James 2:6 with Matthew 5:3; James 5:12 with Matthew 5:34–37; James 1:9 and 4:10 with Matthew 23:12; James 5:17 and Luke 4:25 and so on.

36. James 1:9–11; 2:5–7; 5:1–6.

37. Some examples are Amos 2:6–9; 4:1–6; 5:10–15; 8:4–6; Isaiah 1:17; 3:13–15; 10:1–4; 32:7–8; Jeremiah 2:34; 5:24–29; 7:5–7; 22:3; Habakkuk 3:14; Zechariah 7:8–14.

person in dirty clothes also comes in, and if you take notice of the one wearing the fine clothes and say, "Have a seat here, please," while to the one who is poor you say, "Stand there," or, "Sit at my feet," have you not made distinctions among yourselves, and become judges with evil thoughts? Listen, my beloved brothers and sisters. Has not God chosen the poor in the world to be rich in faith and to be heirs of the kingdom that he has promised to those who love him? But you have dishonored the poor. Is it not the rich who oppress you? Is it not they who drag you into court? Is it not they who blaspheme the excellent name that was invoked over you?

You do well if you really fulfill the royal law according to the scripture, "You shall love your neighbor as yourself." But if you show partiality, you commit sin and are convicted by the law as transgressors. (Jas 2:1–9)

The Roman world at that time, as we saw in chapters 1 and 4 of this book, was a world with extremely sharp class differences. These class differences were not only differences in wealth and power; but even in honor and, in fact, human value. These class differences were built into the very fabric of society: the station into which one was born decided everything about one's life, one's future, and even one's worth as a human being.

However, according to James, these class differences ought to have no place among Christians. In fact, he doubts that one could even be said to believe in Jesus Christ if he accepted the class structure of the Roman world. The reason for this appears evident given what we have already discussed: in declaring the the fulfillment of the promises of Isaiah 58 and 61, promises involving the Jubilee and Sabbatical laws, then in being vindicated as God's Messiah and instituting the new age, Jesus could be seen as having undone the entire institutional framework and ideology of the Roman world. It followed that the class distinctions of the Roman world were to melt away, debts were to be forgiven, and entirely new relationships were to be formed—relationships that had an entirely new foundation. If one was still attached to the class distinctions of the Roman world, how could it be that one really believes in Jesus? Was such a person really keeping oneself unstained by the world (that is, in the context of James's letter, the Roman world)?

The chapter then continues with the famous "faith without works" passage:

What good is it, my brothers and sisters, if you say you have faith but do not have works? Can faith save you? If a brother or sister is naked and lacks daily food, and one of you says to them, "Go in peace; keep warm and eat your fill," and yet you do not supply their bodily needs, what is the good of that? So faith by itself, if it has no works, is dead. (Jas 2:14–17)

Here James continues to insist that the faith a Christian has must result in concrete, material works of righteousness. Notice the term "daily food," which has a parallel (although the Greek terms are different) in the "daily bread" of the Lord's Prayer—it may be that James was teaching that the sharing of food could be the answer to the "daily bread" part of the Lord's Prayer. In the "faith without works" passage, James is telling his readers what faith in God's kingdom ought to look like in practice: it looks like Christian communities sharing and making sure that "not one of them is in need."

The economic practices of the early Christians and their (informal and formal) communism certainly were not spontaneous at all. There was a direct connection between Jesus's declarations, his teachings, the reflections of Christian leaders such as James and John in light of Jesus's death and resurrection; and the economic practices of the Christian communities. Taking into account the teachings of Jesus and the implications of his declaration at the synagogue in Nazareth, along with their vindication in his death and resurrection; it can be said that a community practicing sharing and informal and formal communism would almost be the inevitable outcome. The theology behind these practices were re-enforced, not only by the Gospel writers re-telling Jesus's story, but also by the early Christian leaders through their teachings.

9

A Universal Community

As WE HAVE ALREADY discussed, the most striking feature of the economic practices of the early Christians would not have necessarily been that they practiced forms of informal and formal communism; but that these were practiced cross-culturally, and across ethnic and class lines.

Communities whose economies function primarily on the basis of the principle "from each according to their ability to each according to their need" are not that uncommon in history. However, they are generally found in small groups of neighbors who are held together by a common culture and common interests. Often what ties these individuals together is some kind of kinship, or national or ethnic identity.[1] This makes sense since communism is generally something most naturally practiced among individuals who share a common future and common interests, and who trust one another to a degree. Communism really depends on a basic understanding that each party in the relationship is more or less honest and cares about the welfare of the others to a degree; if that understanding is there, relationships can develop without the added need to quantify and measure everything.[2]

However, the first Christian communities that practiced these forms of communism included individuals who were local Judeans and Galileans as well as Greek-speaking Diaspora Jews.[3] Later on, even non-Jews were admitted into the Christian community.[4] This meant that the community was

1. Fiske, "The Four Elementary Forms of Sociality," 699.
2. Graeber, *Debt*, 34; 104.
3. Acts 6:1–6.
4. Acts 10:44–48.

universal, not ethno-centric. Even so, the socio-economic principles of the Jesus's teachings and the systems of formal and informal communism were still normative for the community; despite the difficulties that would entail (as seen in chapter 6 of this book). Furthermore, there was even sharing between different Christian communities in different parts of the Roman world. For example, there was the collection for the poor in Judea;[5] a collection that Paul was part of and took very seriously.[6] Paul travelled around to different communities collecting funds, and in doing so, he called for an economic equalizing on the basis of Jesus's sacrifice.

The logic for this equalizing (found in Paul's letters to the Corinthians) was that Jesus sacrificed himself, having become poor so that we might become rich—therefore the Corinthians should give up their abundance so that the poorer communities would be less in need and so that there could be a fair balance of wealth between Christian communities. Those in the Corinthian Christian community were expected to share their abundance with other communities, whose members they would likely never meet. Paul then quotes Exodus 16:18, where it is recorded that the Israelites gathered manna in the wilderness and then distributed it so that no one had too much and no one had too little. Paul applies the principle found in Exodus 16:18 to the universal Christian community, from Corinth to Jerusalem.[7]

This is really a unique situation in the ancient world, but one based firmly in Paul's theology. Paul's theology of universal redemption through Christ is summed up nicely in Galatians 3:

> There is no longer Jew or Greek, there is no longer slave or free, there is no longer male and female; for all of you are one in Christ Jesus. And if you belong to Christ, then you are Abraham's offspring, heirs according to the promise. (Gal 3:28–29)

The basic idea here is that the promise to Abraham, that the nations would bless themselves through his seed,[8] had been fulfilled in Christ; therefore men and women from all nations have the possibility of being reconciled to God through Christ—joining the people of God (and thus becoming part of the kingdom of God, with its promises based on the Sabbatical and Jubilee laws, which Christ declared). This gives us the theo-

---

5. Acts 11:29–30; 12:25.

6. Galatians 2:10.

7. 1 Corinthians 16:1–4; 2 Corinthians 8:1–15.

8. Genesis 22:17–18.

logical foundation for Paul's universalism: the idea that membership in the Christian community, and all that comes with it, ought not to be limited by ethnicity, class, or gender.

This theology is found all throughout Paul's letters, especially in his letter to the Romans; where the kingdom of God is universalized to include both Gentiles and Jews brought together through Christ; while at the same time being faithful to the promises of God.

Needless to say, what Paul was doing—as opposed to the Judaizers who appear to have been intent on keeping the Christian community ethnocentric; and in contrast to later groups such as the Marcionites who wanted to completely cut Christianity off from its Jewish roots—was universalizing Christianity; while at the same time holding on to the Jewish idea of an eschatological promise to the people of God. It was this Pauline strand of Christianity that laid the groundwork for a truly universal community based on mutual aid, solidarity, and love: a communism that applied across all ethnic, social, and cultural lines. Paul was doing this entirely on the basis of the idea that through Christ, God had reconciled the world to himself (2 Cor. 5:18–19), an idea that we can also see clearly in Romans 5:

> For while we were still weak, at the right time Christ died for the ungodly. Indeed, rarely will anyone die for a righteous person— though perhaps for a good person someone might actually dare to die. But God proves his love for us in that while we still were sinners Christ died for us. Much more surely then, now that we have been justified by his blood, will we be saved through him from the wrath of God. For if while we were enemies, we were reconciled to God through the death of his Son, much more surely, having been reconciled, will we be saved by his life. But more than that, we even boast in God through our Lord Jesus Christ, through whom we have now received reconciliation. (Rom 5:6–11)

Here we see that the promise given to Israel of restoration and reconciliation—a promise which Jesus claimed was going to be fulfilled in his announcement of the kingdom of God with all of its implications—has not been abandoned; but rather now includes both Jews and Gentiles. This is seen as well in Romans 9:

> It is not as though the word of God had failed. For not all Israelites truly belong to Israel, and not all of Abraham's children are his true descendants; but "It is through Isaac that descendants shall be named for you." This means that it is not the children of the flesh

who are the children of God, but the children of the promise are counted as descendants. (Rom 9:6–8)

. . .

What if God, desiring to show his wrath and to make known his power, has endured with much patience the objects of wrath that are made for destruction; and what if he has done so in order to make known the riches of his glory for the objects of mercy, which he has prepared beforehand for glory—including us whom he has called, not from the Jews only but also from the Gentiles? (Rom 9:22–24)

The chosen people of God, who are to be a part of the eschatological community living out God's kingdom, are the descendants of Abraham as God promised. However, the true descendants of Abraham include both Gentiles and Jews who join the Christian community (as opposed to only the literal blood descendants of Abraham). This results in a truly universal community, one based on love and mutual aid, as we see in Romans 12:

For as in one body we have many members, and not all the members have the same function, so we, who are many, are one body in Christ, and individually we are members one of another. (Rom 12:4–5)

This idea—of breaking the ethno-national barrier and extending the Christian ethic of sharing to people outside the Jewish nation—was not entirely invented by Paul from scratch. The idea goes back to Jesus, as seen specifically, for example, in the parable of the "Good Samaritan":

Just then a lawyer stood up to test Jesus. "Teacher," he said, "what must I do to inherit eternal life?" He said to him, "What is written in the law? What do you read there?" He answered, "You shall love the Lord your God with all your heart, and with all your soul, and with all your strength, and with all your mind; and your neighbor as yourself." And he said to him, "You have given the right answer; do this, and you will live."

But wanting to justify himself, he asked Jesus, "And who is my neighbor?" Jesus replied, "A man was going down from Jerusalem to Jericho, and fell into the hands of robbers, who stripped him, beat him, and went away, leaving him half dead. Now by chance a priest was going down that road; and when he saw him, he passed by on the other side. So likewise a Levite, when he came to the place and saw him, passed by on the other side. But a Samaritan while travel-ing came near him; and when he saw him, he was moved with pity. He went to him and bandaged his wounds, having poured oil and wine on them. Then he put him on his own animal, brought him to an inn, and took care of him. The next day he took out two denarii, gave them to the innkeeper, and said, 'Take care of him; and when I come back, I will repay you whatever more you spend.' Which of these three, do you think, was a neighbor to the man who fell into the hands of the robbers?" He said, "The one who showed him mercy." Jesus said to him, "Go and do likewise." (Luke 10:25–37)

The question being dealt with here is about who one's neighbor is: who is the one to whom I have an ethical obligation?[9] In the context of the Ju-bilee and Sabbatical legislations the neighbor would be the fellow Israelite who would be freed from slavery, have his or her debts forgiven, and have a part of the redistribution involving the return of ancestral lands to their original owners.

In this parable, a man is in need of aid, and a Samaritan (a member of a group of which the Jews were famously disdainful) gives the (presumably Jewish) man the aid that he needed.—Not only immediate aid, the Samari-tan also provided long-term care for the man. This provision of long-term care shows that the Samaritan was prepared to tie himself to being respon-sible for the injured Jew; it was the Samaritan accepting an ethical obli-gation to care for the injured Jew that made that Jew his neighbor. Once someone accepts the obligation to care for someone else, in a sense he is accepting that this person is his neighbor by treating him as such—treating him in such a way that is in sync with the communist ethic "from each ac-cording to his ability, to each according to his need." That is, the Samaritan made himself a neighbor to someone who would normally be his enemy. (Here we see an echo of Jesus's previous teaching to love one's enemies).[10]

This parable takes the general obligation found in the Jewish tradition to love and care for one's neighbor, which includes care for the poor (the widows and orphans);[11] and applies it to literally anyone and everyone in need, even ethnic groups that your own ethnic group considers to be an enemy. When we get to the creation of the first Christian communities, we

9. Leviticus 19:10 is an obvious example of the Jewish obligation to one's neighbor.
10. Luke 6:27–30.
11. For example Exodus 22:25; Leviticus 25:35–36; and Deuteronomy 26:12–14.

see this being put into action, first among Palestinian and Diaspora Jews, then later Samaritans, and then finally Gentiles.[12]

This universalism, to which Jesus hinted and which Paul brought fully to light, was what made Christianity, in principle, the most revolutionary movement in all of history. The Roman Empire and other empires in the past may have been universalist in nature in some way or another, but they were predicated on force and the threat of violence. Various societies in the past were communistic in nature and were based on an ethic of mutual aid and solidarity; but they were predicated on a shared culture, ethnicity, or common interests. It was only with Christianity—specifically Pauline Christianity—that universalism and a communistic ethic of mutual aid and solidarity were brought together in one movement.

This was, and is, extremely counterintuitive. As has already been mentioned, communist relations are generally reserved for neighbors; whereas for strangers one would generally resort to an exchange framework—lest the relationship end up in one party being taken advantage of; or even worse, end up in violence. Yet the Pauline Christians were to act contrary to that intuition and treat people who would otherwise be strangers as though they were kin. Paul was demanding universal solidarity between people that would naturally treat each other as strangers; either by ignoring them, relating to them through an ethic of exchange—an ethic that assumed mutual self-interest—or engaging with them through the threat of violence.[13]

As Paul states again and again in his letters, this universal solidarity is based entirely on the universal messiahship of Jesus Christ—and is realized through his sacrificial death and vindicating resurrection. We can read all Paul's letters in this framework: that of Paul attempting to realize the Jubilee and Sabbatical ideals in Diaspora communities; universalizing what Jesus declared and taught, and what the apostolic community put into practice in Jerusalem.

The Pauline precedent leaves subsequent Christian communities with a challenge. How might the communist ethic that worked in a culturally homogenous community, made up of natural neighbors, be universalized to include other situations? How might individuals, whose cultures would normally separate them, be united—not only in theory, but also in practice—to the point of sharing economic mutual aid and taking on mutual economic obligations toward each other, i.e., communism?

12. Acts 10–11.

13. Greaber, *Anthropological Theory of Value*, 154.

10

A Brief Survey of some other Studies

IN THE SECOND INSTALLMENT of his series "Christianity in the Making",
James Dunn comments on the "community of goods" described in Acts
2:42–47 and Acts 4:32–37:

> Probably we should understand the community of goods in the
> earliest community both as a spontaneous expression of the mu-
> tual affection which their shared experience engendered and as
> an indication that their future horizon was quite limited. In other
> words, they did not plan their communal life-style for the long
> term because they expected the risen and exalted Jesus to return
> soon and the 'restoration of all things'.[1]

John Dominic Crossan, in his book "The Birth of Christianity", gives
his own take on the "community of goods" described in Acts 2:42–47, but
distinguishes it from the Christian communities outside Jerusalem:

> It seems to me, however, that such a title [that of "the poor" given
> to the Christians in Jerusalem in Galatians 2:10] required some
> form of commonality, some type of communal lifestyle, some de-
> gree of difference between the Jerusalem community and other
> Christian communities.[2]

Both of these scholars take the economic practices described in Acts
2 and 4 as a record of something historical, but both of them also limit the
practices in time and scope. James Dunn envisions a spontaneous expression of mutual affection; but he also points out that this expression was to

---

1. Dunn, *Christianity in the Making Vol. 2*, 184.
2. Crossan, *The Birth of Christianity*, 474.

be short lived. The spirit of the moment led to an outpouring of expressions of friendship and sharing, somewhat like a spontaneous celebration. We do not get a picture of a sustained, widespread, intentional, and serious re-arrangement of economic relations based on firm theological grounds; and a building of a strong community of sharing that actually presented a real alternative to the social economy of the Roman world.

John Dominic Crossan sees what happened in Jerusalem as being more or less confined to Jerusalem, an intentional community that was experimenting with a different way of doing things. This was not really an integral part of being Christian; nor a fundamental re-defining of how a Christian is to relate to his or her fellow Christian economically. Rather, it was something more along the lines of an experimental commune.

In my estimation, both of these scholars' views are too limited. When we examine all the evidence—and do so through the lenses of different kinds of social/economic relationships based on competing moral principles; instead of the usual contrasts between communalist versus individualist economics, or private versus public property, or the logic of "economic systems"—we find a picture of the early Christians' "community of goods" that is far richer than what many scholars of early Christianity present.

Along with some historians of early Christianity, many of the commentators on the book of Acts have a difficult time trying to make sense of Acts 2:42–47 and Acts 4:32–37. For example, Catholic scholar J.A. Fitzmyer says in his commentary on Acts:

> *held all things in common.* The sense of this clause is not clear. It could mean that the early Christians pooled all that they owned, or it could mean that they remained owners of property, which they put to the common use of others. The first meaning would make them more like the Essenes, but the second may explain the subsequent stories in chaps. 4 and 5.

> . . .

> What is not wholly clear is the extent to which common ownership was obligatory or voluntary. Even within this passage there is a difference between what is asserted in v 32 about holding all things in common, and the selling of property in v 34, which seems to imply that some members still hold some private property that they can sell.

. . .

> *none of them ever claimed any possession as his own, but they held*
> *all things in common*. This description repeats that of 2:44b, merely
> rephrasing it differently. Nothing is said about how long common
> ownership of property was so practiced, or even how widespread
> it was among Christians. Compare the Greek saying, "Among
> friends everything is common". Luke may well be idealizing the
> situation.[3]

Fitzmyer seems not to know what to make of these accounts. He reads
the "all things in common" passages as addressing the question of property;
and because of this he finds them problematic, and even contradictory. In
the end, he takes the accounts to be perhaps nothing more than an idealization of the situation, implying the practices were short term, localized, limited; and not really to be taken all too seriously. It almost seems as though
Fitzmyer comes across the contradictions, finds no answers to the contradictions—then throws his hands up in despair and suggests that it may all
be a mere idealization. Another Catholic commentary says:

> Even within the summary there emerge two distinct ideas: on the
> one hand, that things were possessed in common in the first com-
> munity (v. 32); on the other hand, that there were individual pos-
> sessors who sold what was theirs for distribution (vv. 34–35). The
> first idea conforms to contemporary Greek ideals of community
> life, whereas the second stands closer to the deuteronomic ideal
> (Dt 15:4, "there shall be no poor among you") and would seem to
> be the original core of the summary. But then again, v. 32 has the
> same interpretation of Christian fellowship (*koinōnia*) in terms of
> a community of goods (*panta koina*) as we encountered in 2:44.
> The redactor apparently developed this idea on the basis of vv.
> 34–35, then combined both notions in 2:44–45.[4]

Here again we see the account being represented as describing two
conflicting practices, a full sharing of goods on the one hand, and an individual selling in order to distribute the proceeds to the poor on the other
hand. His explanation is that the combination of these conflicting practices
was a result of a redactor including these two ideas in one passage without
reconciling them. So the contradiction, according to this commentary, is

---

3. Fitzmyer, *The Acts of the Apostles*, 272.
4. Brown, Fitzmyer, Murphy, *The Jerome Biblical commentary Vol. 2*, 176.

simply a literary mistake. In a commentary written by J.B. Polhill we find something similar:

> Here two ideals for a community of goods seem to be combined. First is the Greek ideal of a community in which everything is held in common and shared equally. It is a basically utopian concept, which can be traced as far back as the Pythagorean communities and is often expressed by the same phrase Luke employed in v. 44, "holding all in common" (*echein hapanta koina*). Verse 45, however, speaks against the early Christian community adopting a practice of community ownership. The imperfect tense is used, indicating that this was a recurrent, continuing practice: their practice was to sell their property and goods and apportion the proceeds whenever a need arose. This is much more in keeping with the Old Testament ideal of community equality, of sharing with the needy so that "there will be no poor among you" (Deut 15:4f.).[5]

Once again, the two practices are set against each other as though they were in conflict—one being a utopian Greek ideal, and the other being an Old Testament ideal.

As to the historical significance of the practices of the Christian community, many commentaries make it very clear that nothing normative is to be taken from these passages. For example I.H. Marshal says:

> The evidence strongly suggests that a feature peculiar to the life of the early church in Jerusalem is being described rather than a universally applicable practice.
>
> The practice in Acts should not be misunderstood. In no sense was it a matter of a rigidly imposed condition upon members of the community. The selling of goods was voluntary, and it was undertaken by the rich.[6]

And in a similar vein K.O. Gangel says:

> Their work also included learning how to live and love together. They sold their possessions and made sure everybody had plenty. Communism? Absolutely not—this was voluntary, contemporary, and discretionary.[7]

These two commentaries, like many others, make it a point to emphasize that the practices were voluntary; and the former makes it clear that

5. Polhill, *Acts,* 120–121.

6. Marshall, *Luke,* 207.

7. Gangel, *Acts,* 31.

they were not to be universally applicable. They both make it clear that they do not think that these passages refer to anything more than discretionary and voluntary charitable giving—the implication is that these passages refer to nothing more than individual philanthropy, not a set of economic practices or a set of social relations. Why do these scholars not see what I see?

One can only speculate, however, I do think there are some fundamental issues underlying many readings of Acts 2:42–47 and Acts 4:32–37 that limit their understanding. One is that many scholars approach these verses with the question of property rights in mind; rather than a question of economic relations. The commentators that see a contradiction between the two practices (holding all things in common, and selling property and distributing the proceeds) tend to think of holding all things in common as describing formal or semi-formal property arrangements; rather than economic relationships based on moral principles that change how one would approach property and how a community would handle the distribution of property.

Another possible culprit for other commentators not seeing what I see is the twentieth-century political conflicts between "socialism" and "capitalism"—which have tended to center around the questions of private property contra public property. This conflict is as old as capitalism itself and is really embedded in the modern consciousness. These political conflicts have infected almost all discussions of economic relationships—both of those who are critical of "capitalism" and from those who defend it. It is very difficult for many people to discuss how people relate to each other economically without (almost through necessity) starting with questions of politics and the state; or to discuss historical phenomena without reading into them modern political concerns. However, if we sidestep those modern political questions, and instead approach the passages primarily using the categories of economic relations and their moral foundations—in the way anthropologists like Alan Fiske or David Graeber would tend to do—rather than property laws or twentieth-century politics; then, as we have seen, we do not have a conflict at all.[8]

Many readings also focus on the "voluntary" nature of the practices. This has to do with a very modern notion of freedom; where economic questions are somehow outside of the realm of obligations—and are consequently answered either by the state, which (in theory) operates

---

8. Greaber, *Anthropological Theory of Value*, 156.

pragmatically for the common good; or are entirely up to the individual to pursue his own aims. These readings assume the notion of freedom where freedom means the pursuit of any end which one may wish to pursue— rather than the freedom to pursue the Good. As we have seen in the previous chapters, this notion of freedom is a modern notion and should not be read back into early Christianity.

The myth of a simplistic self-interested human nature, as exemplified in the famous passage from Adam Smith's Wealth of Nations:

> It is not from the benevolence of the butcher, the brewer, or the baker that we expect our dinner, but from their regard to their own interest. We address ourselves, not to their humanity but to their self-love, and never talk to them of our own necessities but of their advantages.[9]

can lead many readers of Acts 2:42–47 and Acts 4:32–37 to assume a capitalistic framework and then view anything deviating from that as either a completely spontaneous and voluntary departure from the norm, like giving to a beggar; or as necessitating some kind of state or state-like imposition. The field of economics is very much to blame for this myth; much of economics stands on the assumption that everyone is always attempting to maximize their own self-interest—once that assumption is made, then economists can go about atomizing and modeling human behavior (thus they can pretend that the study of human behavior is a science akin to the natural sciences). This economic framework has been internalized by much of the modern culture as being the scientific framework for studying most, if not all, of human behavior. Despite the evidence around us that human beings are not *a priori* always merely self-interested; cynicism about human nature is the assumption in the modern culture's view of economics.[10] This idea of human nature necessarily leads to, and depends on, the idea that human beings naturally deal with each other through an exchange relationship. Since, according to mainstream economics, human beings will always try to maximize their own gain and minimize their own loss—they will therefore naturally deal with, and relate to, others through the mechanisms of barter. The economists assume and insist that the market is some sort of "state of nature" for human society. As David Graeber and other anthropologists have pointed out, this is a modern myth; there is simply no

9. Smith, *The Wealth of nations*, 26–27.
10. Greaber, *Anthropological Theory of Value*, 8.

evidence for a pre-state community where barter was the primary form of distribution.[11] The idea that human beings are first and foremost naturally self-interested has also been shown to be a myth by the field of psychology, "rational choice theory"—assumed by economics—simply does not match up with the way human beings normally operate.[12]

When we drop the assumption of a capitalistic framework things become much easier; we can begin to look at these accounts without assuming that what they are describing must either be private philanthropy or a state-like arrangement of public property—and start to consider that economic relationships can really change simply on the basis of the implementation of new moral foundations in a community. Once we realize that economic relationships are not necessarily morally neutral—we can then look at the early Christians' economic practices as real and normative economic arrangements based on very strong theological and moral imperatives, despite the lack of a state-like enforcement system.

When we read these passages, not with questions of property arrangements in mind; but rather with questions of economic relations in mind—then the supposed contradictions within the text melt away. Reading these passages through the lenses of economic relations makes complete sense of the text; whereas looking at them through the lenses of property arrangements distorts the text and makes it seem self-contradictory. If we really think about it—questions of property have no place in a reconstruction of the early Christian economic practices; questions of property are questions of state law, not questions relevant to something like the Christian *Ekklesia*.

The idea that these practices were localized in Jerusalem and probably only lasted a short time falls apart once we widen our scope to examine more of the evidence. We have seen plenty of evidence in the Pauline letters, the *Didache*, the Church Fathers, as well as non-Christian writers; that these practices lasted through the second century and (in some form at least) beyond, and were known all over the Roman Empire. Due to many unnecessary assumptions, however, such as the focus on property rights, the modern concept of freedom, and the idea that market relationships are built into human nature—there is an impulse to read the accounts of these practices as spontaneous, rare, and non-normative, or even just an idealized fantasy—they just seem far to unrealistic to the modern mind. Thankfully, there is no reason that we ought to bring these assumptions

11. Graeber, *Debt*, 29; 40.

12. Graeber, *Debt*, 90.

into a study of the early Christians; and once we drop those assumptions all the evidence fits together nicely and we have presented before us real, widespread, and long lasting historical economic practices.

These unwarranted assumptions can also cause many readers to tend to not take much of Jesus's teachings that deal with economics found in Luke (much of which is also considered to be part of the theorized Q material, which many scholars take to be some of the earliest material on Jesus) literally. Often, the sayings dealing with debt are interpreted as addressing spiritual sin rather than actual debt relationships; however, there is no reason to push that interpretation (whether true theologically or not) on the earliest listeners and interpreters of those sayings. If we take those sayings at face value, along with the theology of the Jubilee and Sabbatical laws, and the moral teachings found in passages such as the Sermon on the Plain in Luke 6—then the outcome found in Acts 2:42–47 and Acts 4:32–37 comes as much less of a surprise; but rather as, in fact, the logical outcome of Jesus's declarations and teachings.

Conclusion

IN THE PRECEDING CHAPTERS, we have found that the early Christians began to relate to each other in terms of the "from each according to his ability, to each according to his need" logic very early on; and that this way of thinking persisted—even for centuries. We have seen that these practices led to shifting the view of one's own property over to the viewpoint that what one owns ought to be for the benefit of all Christians in need; and that one is obligated to share with one's fellow Christian. We have discovered that this view was so prevalent that the statement by Luke, "they held all things in common," was no idealized hyperbole: the early Christians were actually sharing things to the extent that property lines were blurred to the point of near irrelevancy.

We have learned that the early Christians set up a welfare system; where the moral obligation to share was so strong that the wealthy among them handed over funds sufficient for a regular, systematic distribution to the widows and orphans, and to the poor among them. We have seen evidence for these economic practices from multiple independent sources: from the New Testament itself, to early extra-canonical Christian literature, to the early Church Fathers, and even from non-Christian sources.

We discovered that these changes in economic relationships were found in Christian communities all over the Roman world for centuries, as were the extensive welfare systems. We have seen that these economic practices had a precedent in other Jewish groups such as the Essenes described by Philo, Josephus, and the Dead Sea Scrolls; as well as parallels in Hellenistic philosophical thought and philosophical societies. We have found these economic practices flourishing in a world of brutal, constant, and systematic dispossession of the poor by the Herodian aristocracy, the temple priesthood, and ultimately the Roman authorities; a world saturated with ideologies justifying domination and exploitation. We have also encountered individuals outside of—and critical to—Christianity recognize with puzzlement, mockery, disdain, and sometimes embarrassment the unique economic practices of sharing and care for the poor found within the Christianity of that time.

We have been confronted with difficulties occasioned by these radical changes in the lives and communities of the early Christians that had to be faced; difficulties such as the problem of freeloaders and the tragedy of the commons. We have seen how the early Christians set both moral injunctions and regulations in place in order to prevent those difficulties; all the while maintaining and encouraging the economic practices of mutual aid and sharing, and protecting the institutions of welfare for the poor.

We have seen that, far from being a spontaneous expression of love, far from being some kind of experiment in communal living—these practices were deeply rooted in the declarations and teachings of Jesus and their interpretations by the first Christian leaders. When we look at the full significance of Jesus's declaration in Luke 4:18–19 within the first-century Palestinian context and in light of the second-temple Jewish traditions— we find a call to revolutionize social relationships, to forgive debts, and to redistribute property for the sake of the poor. We also find within Jesus's teachings a framework for working out the ideals of the Sabbatical year law in practice: lending without expectation of return, forgiveness of debts, sharing, and a tying of one's self to one's fellow through mutual obligations.

We see Jesus's apostles taking his declarations and teachings and applying them to the communities that were built on the grounds of Jesus's life, death, and resurrection; resulting in what we see described in Acts 2:42–47 and Acts 4:32–37. Finally, we see in Paul the idea that Jesus's declaration applies, not only to the nation of Israel, but to all who put their faith in Jesus Christ.

All of this becomes clear once we strip away from our thought modern political and economic considerations and categories; as well as modern ideas of individual autonomy, absolute private property, and freedom as mere choice—and we begin to think in the more basic terms of how individuals relate to one another, given specific ideological frameworks and historical contexts; along with the concept of moral obligation.

Christianity was not a doctrine of self-help (either in this life or in an afterlife). The Christianity that developed from the life, teachings, death, and resurrection of Jesus of Nazareth was about reconciling God to humanity, humanity to God and individuals to each other; and revolutionizing how we relate to God and to each other. If Christianity was not concretely changing how people related to one another, socially and economically, then Christianity was not being fully experienced. The ethics of the Jubilee and Sabbatical, as preached by Jesus and practiced by his earliest followers, was central to early Christianity. Those who take on the name Christian must consider its implications in today's ultra-capitalist world if they are to stay true to the spirit of the early Christians.

The ideology of modern Capitalism tends to separate social life from any higher meaning; it tends towards the idea that all social life is nothing more than the management of individual desires—nothing more than a collection of market exchanges between self-interested individuals. Terry Eagleton describes the ideology this way:

> The sway of utility and technology bleach social life of significance, subordinating use-value to the empty formalism of exchange-value. Consumerism by-passes meaning in order to engage the subject subliminally, libidinally, at the level of visceral response rather than reflective consciousness.
>
> . . .
>
> To talk about "significance" and "society" in the same breath just becomes a kind of category mistake, rather like hunting for the hidden meaning of a gust of wind or the hoot of an owl.[1]

This ideology is profoundly anti-Christian.

At the same time without the death of Christ and his resurrection by God as well as man's recognition of the sovereignty of God, the message of solidarity and sharing found within Christianity would have been completely vacuous. Like the Essenes, the Christians believed in the eventual *eschaton*, the judgment of God on the current age, the vindication of God's righteous people, and the resulting vindication of God's sovereignty. Any message of social justice must be a message of God's justice; otherwise it is nothing more than a reflection of a groundless human will. If God is not sovereign, and God's justice is not the final word; then we are left with mere

1. Eagleton, *Ideology,* 37–38.

worldly power, domination, and alienation. The *eschaton* is the *protasis* to the *apodosis* of the *koinōnia*, the former causes the latter, and the latter is contingent on the former.

Earlier, we discussed the story of Cain and Abel; in that story a very important question came up:

> Then the Lord said to Cain, "Where is your brother Abel?" He said, "I do not know; am I my brother's keeper?" (Gen 4:9)

Cain asked this question to God; but God did not directly answer the question right then and there. In a sense, this question is still very much alive: does one have an intrinsic obligation to care for one's fellow? Unfortunately, this question is often dealt with by assuming, *a priori*, that there is no intrinsic obligation to one's neighbor; and then trying to figure out the best way to run a society from a utilitarian standpoint. This often leads to the situation of different groups fighting for their own interests, trying to model society in a way that gets their group a larger piece of the pie. Alternatively, it ends with just answering "no", and then figuring out a way human beings can best pursue their own individual interests un-restrained. What is lacking in these modern conversations is what Jesus and the early Christians first took into account: God's will.

The early Christians understood that how one deals with one's neighbor is entirely dependent on how one relates to God and God's kingdom. Cain's question was rightly addressed to God, not to any fellow man or to himself. We are created by God in his image and thus our obligations to each other are dependent on, and determined by, God. Jesus and his followers answered Cain's question with a resounding "yes"—we are our brother's and sister's keepers. While the ideological descendants of Cain followed his example of violence and, according to Josephus, reducing economic relations to market exchange, property accumulation, and profiteering; the first Christians followed the course of the Jubilee and Sabbatical ethical framework—sharing freely, lending without account, and sacrificing for each other; creating real communist relationships.

It is unfortunate that Christians have often ignored the question brought up by Cain; and that those who do address that question often ignore the fundamental question of God. The question brought up by Cain is central to Christian theology, and it cannot be fully answered outside of the acknowledgement of God. Basil of Caesarea put it beautifully:

"But whom do I treat unjustly," you say, "by keeping what is my own?" Tell me, what is your own? What did you bring into this life? From where did you receive it? It is as if someone were to take the first seat in the theater, then bar everyone else from attending, so that one person alone enjoys what is offered for the benefit of all in common—this is what the rich do. They seize common goods before others have the opportunity, then claim them as their own by right of preemption. For if we all took only what was necessary to satisfy our own needs, giving the rest to those who lack, no one would be rich, no one would be poor, and no one would be in need. (Basil of Caesarea, *Sermon to the Rich* [Schroeder])

Basil forces us to acknowledge that ultimately, everything comes from God and is given to mankind in common. To ask about whether or not we have a right to dominate creation to the detriment of others, and what our obligation is to others—is to ask the question of creation. If we are nothing more than an interesting collection of atoms; with no creator, no purpose, no obligations, no intrinsic value; if creation is not a gift to us by our and its creator—then there is no reason why we should not dominate all we can to the detriment of whomever: there are no obligations for us to fulfill. If, however, we are created in the image of God and if creation is a free gift to humankind; then we are obligated to reflect and recognize our creator.

The Christian message is that humankind has not only failed in that obligation, but rebelled against it; however, it is also that God sent his Messiah to fulfill that obligation and to release us from the debt of sin. Those who recognized that message from the start went on to put into practice its social implications: to hold all things in common, keeping fellowship with each other and with God.

Putting the economic teachings of Jesus, based on the principles of the Jubilee and Sabbatical laws, into practice was not optional for the early Christians; it was not something that a Christian might do if he or she feels like being an especially nice person. This was something that a Christian must do, was obligated to do; it was just as central to the early Christians as was refraining from idolatry and fornication. In fact, not to give of one's means to the common good may be likened to theft according to John Chrysostom:

This also is robbery—not to impart our good things to others. Very likely it may seem to you a strange saying; but wonder not at it, for I will, from the Divine Scriptures, bring testimony showing that not only robbery of other men's goods, but also the not imparting our own good things to others,—that this also is robbery, and covetousness, and fraud. What then is this testimony? God, rebuking the Jews, speaks thus through the prophet: "The earth has brought forth her fruit, and ye have not brought in the tithes; but the plunder of the poor is in your houses," (Mal. iii. 10.) Since, it is said, ye have not given the customary oblations, ye have robbed the poor. This is said in order to show to the rich that they possess things which belong to the poor, even if their property be gained by inheritance,—in fact, from what source so ever their substance be derived. And, again, in another place, it is said, "Do not deprive the poor of life," (Ecclus. iv. 1.) Now, he who *deprives,* deprives some other man of property. It is said to be deprivation when we retain things taken from others. And in this way, therefore, we are taught that if we do not bestow alms, we shall be treated in the same way as those who have been extortioners. (Chrysostom, *Discourse on the parable of the Rich man and Lazarus,* 2.4 [Allen])

It is common today that people separate their economic lives from their religious lives. The phrase "it's not personal, it's just business" reflects that attitude. Christianity does not allow such a distinction. Christianity is about the kingdom of God and the working out of the Jubilee and Sabbatical ideals both in the here and now as well as in the *eschaton.* Christianity is about the renewal of everything—everything is God's business—including our approach to how we relate to one another. The question of bringing about social justice in the economy is also, necessarily, a religious one—since it is a question of justice; and justice is ultimately dependent entirely on God: the source of justice.

The earliest Christians held all things in common not claiming anything as their own, and not one of them was in need—and they did so because of Jesus's declarations and teachings.

πνεῦμα κυρίου ἐπ' ἐμὲ οὗ εἴνεκεν ἔχρισέν με εὐαγγελίσασθαι πτωχοῖς, ἀπέσταλκέν με, κηρύξαι αἰχμαλώτοις ἄφεσιν καὶ τυφλοῖς ἀνάβλεψιν, ἀποστεῖλαι τεθραυσμένους ἐν ἀφέσει, κηρύξαι ἐνιαυτὸν κυρίου δεκτόν.

. . .

καὶ οὐδὲ εἷς τι τῶν ὑπαρχόντων αὐτῷ ἔλεγεν ἴδιον εἶναι ἀλλ' ἦν αὐτοῖς ἅπαντα κοινά.

. . .

οὐδὲ γὰρ ἐνδεής τις ἦν ἐν αὐτοῖς·

Bibliography

"A Messianic Apocalypse." In *The Complete Dead Sea Scrolls in English—Revised Edition,* Translated by Geza Vermes. London: Penguin, 2012.

"Covenant of Damascus." In *The Complete Dead Sea Scrolls in English—Revised Edition,* Translated by Geza Vermes. London: Penguin, 2012.

"Manual of Discipline." In *The Complete Dead Sea Scrolls in English—Revised Edition,* Translated by Geza Vermes. London: Penguin, 2012.

"The Didache." In *The Apostolic Fathers in English.* Translated by Michael W. Holmes. Ada: Baker, 2006.

"The Epistle of Barnabas." In *The Apostolic Fathers in English.* Translated by Michael W. Holmes. Ada: Baker, 2006.

"The Heavenly Prince Melchizedek." In *The Complete Dead Sea Scrolls in English—Revised Edition,* Translated by Geza Vermes. London: Penguin, 2012.

Aristotle. *The Nicomachean Ethics.* Translated by William David Ross. Oxford: Clarendon, 1908.

Badiou, Alain. *The Communist Hypothesis.* Translated by David Macey and Steve Corcoran. London: Verso, 2010.

Basil of Caesarea. "Sermon to the Rich." In *On Social Justice.* Translated by C.P. Schroeder. Yonkers: St. Vladimirs Seminary Press, 2009.

Bauckham, Richard. "James and the Jerusalem Community." In *Jewish Believers in Jesus: The Early Centuries,* edited by Oskar Skarsaune and Reidar Hvalvik. Peabody: Hendrickson, 2007.

Brown, Peter. *Through the Eye of a Needle: Wealth, the Fall of Rome, and the Making of Christianity in the West,* 350–550 AD. Princeton: Princeton University Press, 2013.

Brown, R. E. and Fitzmyer, J. A. and Murphy, R. E., *The Jerome Biblical commentary Vol. 2.* Englewood Cliffs: Prentice-Hall, 1992.

Capper, Brian. "The Palestinian Cultural Context of Earliest Christian Community of Goods." In *The Book of Acts: Vol. 4 Palestinian Settings,* edited by Richard Bauckham. Grand Rapids: Eerdmans, 1995.

Carter, Warren. "Matthew's People." In *A Peoples History of Christianity: Christian Origins,* edited by David Horsley. Minneapolis: Fortress Press, 2005.

Cicero. *Cicero Vol. 11: On Duties*. Translated by Walter Miller. Cambridge: Harvard University Press, 1913.

Clement of Alexandria. "The Instructor." In *Ante-Nicene Fathers Vol. 2*. Translated by Alexander Roberts and James Donaldson. Peabody: Hendrickson, 1994.

Crawford, Robert G. *What Is Religion? Introducing the Study of Religion*. Abingdon: Routledge, 2002.

Crossan, John Dominic. *The Birth of Christianity: Discovering What Happened in the Years Immediately After the Execution of Jesus*. New York: Harpercollins, 2010.

Diogenes Laertius. *Lives of the Eminent Philosophers Vol. 1*. Translated by Robert Drew Hicks. New York: Putnam's, London: Heinemann, 1925.

Dunn, James D. *Jesus Remembered: Christianity in the Making Vol. 1*. Grand Rapids: Eerdmans, 2003.

————. *Beginning from Jerusalem: Christianity in the Making Vol. 2*. Grand Rapids: Eerdmans, 2008.

Eagleton, Terry. *Ideology: An Introduction*. London: Verso, 1991.

Eusebius. *Praeparatio Evangelica*. Translated by E.H. Gifford. Oxford: Oxford Univeristy Press, 1903.

Evans, Craig. *From Jesus to the Church: The First Christian Generation*. Louisville: Westminster John Knox, 2007.

Ferguson, Everett. *Backgrounds of Early Christianity*. Grand Rapids: Eerdmans, 2003.

Fiensy, David A. "The Composition of the Jerusalem Church." In *The Book of Acts: Vol. 4 Palestinian Settings*, edited by Richard Bauckham. Grand Rapids: Eerdmans, 1995.

Fiske, Alan. "The Four Elementary Forms of Sociality—Framework for a Unified "Theory of Social Relations." *Psychological Review* Vol. 99 No. 4 (1992) 689–723.

————. *Structures of Social Life*. London: Macmillan, 1991.

Fitzmyer, Joseph A. T*he Acts of the Apostles: a new translation with introduction and commentary*. New Haven: Yale University press, 2008.

Freyne, Sean. "Galilee and Judea in the first century." In *The Cambridge History of Christianity Vol. 1: Origins to Constantine*, edited by Margaret M. Mitchel and Frances M. Young. Cambridge: Cambridge University Press, 2014.

Gangel, Kenneth. *Holman New Testament Commentary—Acts*. Nashville: Broadman & Holman Publishers, 1998.

Graeber, David. *Debt: the first 5000 years*. Brooklyn: Melville House, 2015.

————. *Toward and Anthropological Theory of Value: The False Coin of our own Dreams*. New York: Palgrave, 2001.

Hardin, Garrett. "The Tragedy of the Commons." *Science magazine* Vol. 162, No. 3859 (December 13 1998) 1243–1248.

Hart, David Bentley. *Atheist Delusions: The Christian Revolution and its fashionable Enemies*. New Haven: Yale University Press, 2009.

Herzog II, William R. "Why Peasants Responded to Jesus." In *A Peoples History of Christianity: Christian Origins*, edited by David Horsley. Minneapolis: Fortress, 2005.

Horsley, David. "Jesus Movements and the Renewal of Israel." In *A Peoples History of Christianity: Christian Origins*, edited by David Horsley. Minneapolis: Fortress, 2005.

Huffman, Carl. "Pythagoras." In *Stanford Encyclopaedia of Philosophy*. https://plato.stanford.edu/entries/pythagoras/.

Hume, Douglas A. *The Early Christian Community: A Narrative Analysis of Acts 2:41–47 and 4:32–35*. Tübingen: Mohr Siebeck, 2011.

BIBLIOGRAPHY

Ignatius. "Letter to the Smyrnaeans." In *The Apostolic Fathers in English*. Translated by Michael W. Holmes. Ada: Baker, 2006.

Irenaeus, "Against Heresies." In *Ante-Nicene Fathers Vol. 1*. Translated by Alexander Roberts and William Rambaut. New York: Christian Literature Co., 1885.

John Chrysostom. *Four Discourses of Chrysostom, chiefly on the parable of the Rich man and Lazarus*. Translated by F. Allen, B.A. London: Longmans, 1869.

Josephus. "Antiquities." In *The Works of Josephus, Complete and Unabridged New Updated Edition*. Translated by William Whiston and A. M. Peabody. Hendrickson, 1987.

————. "War of the Jews." In *The Works of Josephus, Complete and Unabridged New Updated Edition*. Translated by William Whiston. Peabody: Hendrickson, 1987.

Julian the Apostate. "Letter 22 to Arsacius, High–priest of Galatia." In *The Works of the Emperor Julian Vol. 3*. Translated by W. C. Wright. New York: Putnam's, London: Heinemann, 1913.

————. "Letter 40." In *The Works of the Emperor Julian Vol. 3*. Translated by W. C. Wright. New York: Putnam's, London: Heinemann, 1913.

Justin Martyr. "First Apology." In *Ante-Nicene Fathers Vol 1*. Translated by Alexander Roberts and James Donaldson. Peabody: Hendrickson, 1994.

Lowe, Bruce A. "Paul, Patronage and Benefaction: A "Symbiotic" Reconsideration." In *Paul and his Social Relations,* edited by Stanley E. Porter and Christopher D. Land. Leiden: Brill, 2012.

Lucian. "The Passing of Peregrinus." In *Lucian Vol. 5*. Translated by A.M. Hamron. New York: Putnam's, London: Heinemann, 1925.

Malina, Bruce J. and Pilch, John J. *Social-Science Commentary on the Book of Acts*. Minneapolis: Fortress, 2008.

————. *Social-Science Commentary on the Book of Revelation*. Minneapolis: Fortress, 2000.

Malina, Bruce J. *The New Jerusalem in the Revelation of John: The City as Symbol of Life with God*. Collegeville: Liturgical, 2000.

Marshall, Howard I. *Luke: historian and theologian*. Exeter: Paternoster, 1970.

Marx, Karl. *Critique of the Gotha Program*. London: International, 1928.

Mauss, Marcel. *The Gift: The Form and Reason for Exchange in Archaic Societies*. Abingdon: Routledge, 2002.

Meyes, Eric and Chancey, Mark. *Alexander to Constantine: Archaeology of the Land of the Bible*. New Haven: Yale University Press, 2009.

Morley, Neville. "The Poor in the city of Rome." In *Poverty in the Roman World,* edited by Atkins, Margaret and Osborne, Robin. Cambridge: Cambridge University Press, 2006.

Nicols, John. "Hospitality among the Romans." In *The Oxford Handbook of Social Relations in the Roman World,* edited by Michael Peachin. Oxford: Oxford University Press, 2014.

Origen. "Against Celsus." In *Ante-Nicene Fathers Vol. 9*. Translated by Alexander Roberts and James Donaldson. Peabody: Hendrickson, 1994.

Osiek, Carolyn. "The Social Sciences and the Second Testament: Problems and Challenges, Biblical Theology," *Bulletin* 22.2 (1992) 88–95.

Parkin, Anneliese. "'You do him no Service': another exploration of pagan almsgiving." In *Poverty in the Roman World,* edited by Atkins, Margaret and Osborne, Robin. Cambridge: Cambridge University Press, 2006.

Philo. "On the Embassy to Gaius." In *The Works of Philo: Complete and Unabridged.* Translated by Charles Duke Yonge. Peabody: Hendrickson, 1993.

Plato. "Gorgias." In *Plato in Twelve Volumes Vol.* 3. Translated by W.R.M. Lamb. Cambridge: Harvard University Press, 1925.

———. "Protagoras." In *Plato in Twelve Volumes Vol.* 2. Translated by W.R.M. Lamb. Cambridge: Harvard University Press, 1925.

Pliny the Younger. "Book 10 letter 96 to the Emperor Trajan." In *The Letters of Pliny the Younger.* Translated by Betty Radice. London: Penguin, 1975.

Polhill, John. *Acts: An Exegetical and Theological Exposition of Holy Scripture.* Nashville: Broadman & Holman, 1992.

Seneca. "On Benefits." In *Moral Essays Vol.* 3. Translated by John W. Basore. Cambridge: Harvard University Press, 1935.

Smith, Adam. *An Inquiry into the Nature and Causes of the Wealth of Nations, Volume* 1. Oxford: Oxford University Press, 1976.

Stark, Rodney. *The Triumph of Christianity: How the Jesus Movement Became the World's Largest Religion.* New York: Harpercollins, 2011.

Stevenson, Leslie and Haberman, David L. and Wright, Peter Matthews. *Twelve Theories of Human Nature.* Oxford: Oxford University Press, 2013.

Taylor, Charles. *A Secular Age.* Cambridge: Harvard University Press, 2007.

Tertullian. "Apology." In *Ante-Nicene Christian Library Vol.* 11. Translated by S. Thelwall. Edinburgh: T&T Clark, 1869.

Titus Maccius Plautus. "Trinummus." In *The Comedies of Plautus.* Translated by Henry Thomas Riley. London: G. Bell & Sons, 1912.

Verboven, Koenraad. "Friendship among the Romans." In *The Oxford Handbook of Social Relations in the Roman World,* edited by Michael Peachin. Oxford: Oxford University Press, 2014.

Ward, Keith. *The Case for Religion.* London: Oneworld, 2004.

Witherington, Ben. *The Acts of the Apostles: A Socio-Rhetorical Commentary.* Grand Rapids: Eerdmans, 1997.

Woolf, Greg. "Writing Poverty in Rome." In *Poverty in the Roman World,* edited by Atkins, Margaret and Osborne, Robin. Cambridge: Cambridge University Press, 2006.

Wright, N.T. *Acts for Everyone Part* 1: *Chapters* 1–12. London: SPCK, 2008.

Yoder, John Howard, *The politics of Jesus.* Grand Rapids: Eerdmans, 2004.

Ancient Document Index

DEAD SEA SCROLLS

GRECO-ROMAN WRITINGS